INCIDENT MANAGEMENT PROCESS GUIDE FOR INFORMATION TECHNOLOGY

CARLO FIGLIOMENI, B.B.M.

To order additional copies of this book, contact:
Xlibris
844-714-8691
www.Xlibris.com
Orders@Xlibris.com

ISBN: Softcover   979-8-3694-0851-3
             EBook   979-8-3694-0850-6

Library of Congress Control Number: 2023918817

Print information available on the last page

Rev. date: 10/10/2023

Table of Contents

1   Preface

1.1 Introduction

Industry defines a Process as the act of taking something through an established and usually routine approved set of procedures to convert it from one form to another. A process involves pre-defined steps, roles, and responsibilities, defined accountability of situation owner in the decision-making process to accomplish the task on hand. Based on the definition.

- To understand what the Incident Management process is; read the ITIL Incident Management documentation.
- To understand the content required for the auditability of the Incident Management process; read the CobiT module DS8 documentation.
- To understand who, what, when and how to implement the Incident Management process continue reading this book.

This book is the result of years, spent in detailing and actual conducting the Incident process, in providing organization transformation guidance on Information Technology Infrastructure Library (**ITIL ®**)[1] and Control Objectives for Information and related Technology (**CobiT ®**)[2] mandate module DS8 – Manage Incidents. This book can be used by any organization who wants to implement and manage a robust Incident Management Process to deliver quality service by providing quality service to their customers.

The book is designed so that it can be used by either an existing Incident Management Manager, who wants to improve the way Incidents are handled to reduce the impact to their customers, or by any organization that is planning to introduce a formal Incident Management Process within their environment; - being Information Technology group or any other Business group.

---

1   *ITIL ® is a Registered Trademark, and a Registered Community Trademark of the Office of Government Commerce and is registered in the U.S. Patent and Trademark Office".*

2   *The IT Governance Institute® (ITGI) was established in 1998 to advance international thinking and standards in directing and controlling and enterprise's information technology.*

2　Document Overview

2.1 Introduction

The purpose of this document is to describe the Incident Management process that will be used across the organization. This document is intended to function as a reference guide that outlines the relevant activities, roles & responsibilities, policies, and reference data required to facilitate the identification, and timely and accurate resolution of incidents associated with the production baseline.

> **Note:** The process may exclude issues related to Project Incident prior to implementation into production. Until transitioned to the support team, these incidents are handled via the existing Change Management process and Project PIR (Post Implementation Review), managed by the Project Manager in coordination with the Change Manager and appropriate project and support staff.
>
> Project activities prior to being transition to production do not go through the established ITS Incident Process.

The process improvement efforts for the Incident Management Process Guide should be carried out according to Company ABXYZ wide vision, policies, process improvement methodologies, and practices.

The **Incident[3] Management** process focuses on the rapid restoration of services following an unplanned deviation within the environment. In tandem, Incident Management also focuses on managing the day-to-day support interface and service request handling between clients[4] and service providers.

3　Any event that is not part of the standard operation of a service and that causes, or may cause, an interruption to, or a reduction in, the quality of that service.

4　Whenever the term 'clients' is used it includes Information Technology, Internal and External customers.

3   Process Overview

The Incident Management process performs an essential role in maintaining the overall stability and quality of the Information Technology Services (ITS) Operation Management. The key focus is on restoring service operations as quickly as possible following an unexpected service deviation.

3.1 Definitions

Incident Management comprises two major components.

1. 'Service Interruption'- The operational process designed to respond to support requirements to enable service delivery as soon as possible. The customer's expectation is to experience minimal service disruption. In case of a disruption the service must be restored as quickly as possible to resume normal work activities.
    a. A service interruption is any event which is not part of the standard daily operation of a service, and which causes, or may cause, an interruption to, or a reduction in the quality of that contracted service, as per agreed commitment levels. This could be reported by Clients or Automation.

2. 'Service Request'- The ability to allow the business to request new services which are not part of the existing daily service agreed to.
    a. Service Request encompasses the provision of new services required that are delivered through agreed procedures and have require appropriate approvals. This could be anything that the business has deem necessary to accommodate their needs, such as.

        i. New or modified report,
        ii. Changes to existing data receipts
        iii. New functions and services

These types of incidents are referred to as 'Service Interruption' and 'Service Request', respectively, to allow for the different processes and support teams that are involved in their resolution.

A Major Incident is a significant IT operational event (Service Interruption) leading to a severe impact on the Client Community, or where the disruption is excessive in duration and the result will jeopardizes the service commitment targets already agreed or it may be visible to Senior Management.

The Major Incident Process leverages similar management and resolution activities required in the restoration of the service interruption. The primary difference between an Incident and a Major Incident pertains to the increased rate of activity required in the recover execution and monitoring, and keeping the stakeholder and the management notified of action is currently taking place, the status and expected outcome.

3.2 Mission Statement

The mission of Incident Management is to facilitate the quality and fast successful restoration of IT service to the customers, as defined within each service level agreement.

3.3 Goal Statement

The primary goal of the Incident Management process is to restore normal service operation as quickly as possible and minimize the adverse impact on business operations, thus ensuring that the best possible levels of service quality and availability are maintained. 'Normal service operation' is defined here as service operation within the Service Level Agreement (SLA) parameters. The primary activities to achieve this goal are:

- To attempt to resolve incidents during the first call with the user.
- To ensure accurate and consistent logging of incident tickets
- To assign incidents to technical support groups accurately
- To ensure that the users are satisfied with the resolution of incidents.
- To produce management information that can be leveraged to continuously improve the process.

3.4 Objectives

The objectives of the Incident Management process are:

- Develop and maintain meaningful records relating to every incident created.
- Own and control all incidents (track and monitor)
- Prompt incident resolution through optimal usage of support resources and technologies
- Communicate incident status to all concerned parties via the Service Desk
- Initiate escalation as required to obtain resolution as per known agreements.
- Ensure optimal resource utilization in supporting the business.

3.5 Scope

The following section outlines the scope of the Incident Management process within the ITS organization:

Activity Scope

IS	IS NOT
Incident identification and recording (User Initiated or via Event Monitoring)	A request for a new service (Incidents are confined to existing, defined services)
Classification and initial support of the incident	Management and execution of root cause analysis activities (some coverage of this will be included in Postmortem in the absence of Problem Management process).
Investigation and diagnosis of the incident	To always provide a permanent / structural solution. A workaround may be sufficient.
Incident resolution and service restoration	The operational procedures followed by a support team to effect technical resolution.
Communicating with the customer and closing the incident	Closing the incident without the client approval.

Operation Management

Incidents:

- A detected Operation Management event (e.g., alerts monitored by software)
- A user reported service disruption (e.g., an application is not behaving as it should)

Service Requests:

In Scope Service Requests, for example, consists of:

o Moves, adds, deletes, changes (user IDs, PC's, Printers, Servers, Cable change requests).

- A Customer request for information – Service Request.
- Password resets / lockouts.
- ID lockouts.
- Batch schedule changes.
- Operational parameter change (Depends on object being changed).
- Product assistance (How to's).
- Requests for software installations.
- Requests for additional outputs (reports).
- Telephony service requests.
- Procurement Requests.
- Requests for Training
- Hardware Service Request.
- Data Restoration (Backup / Restore).
- Domain Name System (DNS) Service Requests – Record a name change.
- Requests for remote access capabilities – problems with remote access.
- Requests for special reports.
- To check a device does not contain any virus prior to being introduced into the Environment.
- Special Needs Requests - Disability Requirements.
- New Projects
- New product and service introduction activities
- Infrastructure development activities
- Major platform, Hardware, and Operating System changes
- New revisions of software
- Ongoing business support (i.e., new applications or service definitions)
- Problem resolution (Distinct from incident resolution)
- Resource request (asking for resources)

Out of Scope Service Requests:

- Requests made to ITS that do not follow the established Service Request process.

4   Roles & Responsibilities

This section describes the roles and corresponding responsibilities that have been defined for the Incident Management process.

4.1 Incident Management Process Owner

Role Description

The Incident Management Process Owner provides process leadership to the ITS organization by overseeing the process and ensuring that the process is followed by the organization. The Incident Management Process Owner has the accountability and authority for the overall process results.

Responsibilities

- Ensures that the process is defined, documented, maintained & communicated at an enterprise and local level.
- Defines Incident Management Team roles, responsibilities, and accountabilities.
- Defines and communicates the mission, process, workflow, policies, and rules.
- Represents the Incident Management process to all external groups.
- Accountable for compliance, overall performance, and results of the process
- Defines and develops Incident Management process common metrics and reporting requirements.
- Reviews effectiveness and efficiency of the Incident Management process and identifies opportunities for process improvement.
- Gains commitment at an executive level for the resources and responsibilities needed to ensure the process is effective.
- Responsible for regular Incident Management continuous improvement process meetings
- Reviews feedback to gauge customer satisfaction with the process
- Controls and leads process improvement.
- Approves or rejects process deviation requests.
- Facilitates, resolves, or escalates cross-functional issues.
- Ensures organizational adherence to the process.
- Ensures adequate process training is available for the organization.
- Responsible to define data and functional requirements of the Incident Management tool.
- Ensures Incident Management processes and tools integrate with other ITIL processes and tools.
- Manages changes to the process within a defined governance framework. This includes reviewing and approving all proposed changes and communicating changes to all the participants and affected areas.
- Is responsible for the success or failure of the process and has the authority to represent management on common process definition decisions

4.2 Incident Manager

Role Description

The Incident Manager is responsible for the operational quality and integrity of Incident Management process activities. The Incident Manager is ultimately accountable for all Incidents and is the primary Incident Management escalation point.

Responsibilities/Tasks

- Oversees the day-to-day execution of the Incident Management process.
- Manages ITS support staff performance of the Incident Management process, creates, and executes action plans when necessary to ensure continuous improvement.
- Acts as focal point for process communication with clients, service providers, and management.
- Responds to process exceptions and deviations.
- Ensures completeness and integrity of information collected to conduct daily operations.
- Ensures availability of defined Incident Management reports
- Chairs Incident Review meetings
- Notifies the participants in the Incident Management process when standards and procedures are not being followed.
- Recommends process improvements to the Incident Management Process Owner
- Implements approved changes to the process and Incident Management reporting.
- Communicates new and changed policies.
- Identifies and responds to Incident Management process training requirements.
- Issues briefing notes to the executive management team.
- Accountable for Postmortem execution and results
- Accountable for monitoring progress and completion of Postmortem action items
- Oversees the MIT progress to ensure, in case of multiple MIT, they are proceeding accordingly.

4.3 Incident Coordinator

Role Description

The Incident Coordinator functions as the primary focal point for Severity 1 & 2 incidents while in tandem coordinating the process execution, resource identification, and postmortem activities.

Responsibilities/Tasks

- Coordinates the execution of the Major Incident process.
- Confirms the validity and scope of a Major Incident
- Ensures that each Major Incident is assigned an Incident Coordinator and is responded to within the appropriate time frame.
- Identify technical support resources (Major Incident Team)
- Ensures that internal notification and escalation activities are executed.
- Facilitates and coordinates business impact mitigation efforts.
- Act as focal point for process execution and communication with clients, service providers, and management
- Ensures that the customer has confirmed that the service has been restored to the customer's satisfaction (for incidents reported by the customer)
- Ensures the progress of the Major Incident recovery are documented in the associated incident record.
- Participate in the Major Incident meeting.
- Assist Incident Manager with the initiation and coordination of postmortem activities.

4.4 Queue Manager

Role Description

The Queue Manager role is applicable to both the Service Desk (Tier 1) and Tier 2 support groups. The role is responsible for addressing process execution issues encountered by support personnel and ensuring that all tickets assigned to a Queue are promptly addressed.

Responsibilities/Tasks

- Monitors the incident Queues.
- Ensures that all tickets assigned to a Queue are retrieved OR routed to the appropriate resource.
- Ensures that each incident is assigned to an Incident Analyst or Incident Agent
- Monitors all incidents and advises support group of upcoming and actual Service Level Breaches (Note: Engaging support group will only occur if Incident Agent has not performed this action)
- Responds to the escalated issues in a timely and appropriate fashion to minimize the effect of incidents on agreed service levels.
- Follows defined escalation path, as defined in the escalation directives.
- Facilitates resolution of issues that do not comply with the process.
- Facilitates support resource commitment and allocation.
- Attends incident review meetings.
- Reviews Incident Management metrics and reporting and takes action to address areas where performance is weak.
- Participates in process improvement sessions

4.5 Incident Analyst

Role Description

The Incident Analyst, usually a 2nd line support professional, is the subject matter expert of his/her competency domain(s). He/she is responsible to quickly provide a comprehensive analysis of an incident and/or a solution to restore the disrupted service as soon as possible. Incident Analysts are members of the Major Incident team, when the service they are accountable for is disrupted.

Responsibilities/Tasks

- Determines what is required to restore the service and initiates the appropriate action. The actions may include:
  - Consulting with the user as required to confirm symptoms and gather further information.
  - Invoking additional technical resources as necessary, internal or third party
  - Initiating a request for change
  - Creating a workaround
  - Executing a workaround or resolution
  - Validation of the success of workaround or resolution, at least from a technical perspective
- Executes according to service levels.
- Functionally escalates to higher levels of support in accordance with applicable resolution thresholds.
- Keeps first-level support always informed.
- Review and validate the scope of Major Incidents throughout its lifecycle.
- Keep the Incident Manager updated of the status on all high severity incidents.
- Updates the incident ticket with status, actions, and final resolution information.
- Provides effective resolution to incidents in accordance with the severity service level.
- Identifies resolved incidents as candidates for inclusion in the Knowledge Repository
- Provides knowledge and training to first level support

4.6 Incident Agent

Role Description

Performed By: Service Desk Agent

The Incident Agent, being in most instances the 1st line support professional, is the primary contact person for the customers and functions as a hub between the business unit and the ITS organization. He/she is in most cases the owner of the incidents and therefore responsible for creating the incident tickets and coordinating their resolution.

Performed By: Computer Operation for after hours support.

The Incident Agent, being in most instances the 1st line support professional, is the primary contact person for Operation Management generated incident. He/she is in most cases the owner of the incidents and therefore responsible for creating the incident tickets and coordinating their resolution. The Service Desk is notified of incidents that impact service.

Responsibilities/Tasks

- Receives contact from user by phone, email, or other authorized means.
- Collects contact and request information from user.
- Opens new or updates existing tickets.
- Identifies and applies updates to the CMDB (if in place)
- Classifies and categorizes the incident (based on SLA parameter)
- Notifies Incident Coordinator when a potential Severity 1 incident has been detected.
- Resolves request by attempting to find a solution / workaround match within knowledge management system.
- Identifies appropriate ticket associations.
- Assigns unresolved requests to the appropriate support group Subject Matter Expert
- Ensures assigned tickets are handled appropriately during off shift, turn over ongoing activities to on site Agent.
- Upon request, informs the user of the status of an existing request.
- Confirms request status and resolution with user.
- Determines user satisfaction with request handling.
- Initiates escalations.
- Monitors incidents and advises support group of upcoming and actual Service Level Breaches
- Closes incidents

Incident Agent - Responsibilities/Tasks (Continued)

[SUB ROLE – INCIDENT AGENT (LEAD SME)] (Also Responsible for performing all the above activities)

- Provides in-depth knowledge of specific application / service / infrastructure component.
- Functions as first escalation point for unresolved incidents related to a specific support Queue.
- Provides validation and / or confirmation of incident dispatch.
- Ensures all relevant stakeholders within their support Queue are engaged in the process, as required.
- Provides support Queue specific process communication and training.
- Identifies process issues within and outside their department and recommends improvements to the Team Lead

4.7 ITS Management

Role Description

ITS Management is responsible to support the Major Incident process by authorizing additional resources to facilitate resolution. In addition, the management team enforces postmortem activity adherence through the review and approval of action items.

Responsibilities

- Manage internal and cross functional escalation issues.
- Approve briefing notes.
- Participate in monthly Major Incident review meetings.
- Participate in Postmortem summary meetings.
- Review and approve Postmortem detailed analysis reports.
- Upon request, provide Major Incident status updates to Business Unit and ITS Management team.
- Investigate and manage customer satisfaction issues

5   Detailed Process Description

5.1 High Level Process Flow

Incident Management Process High Level Logic flow.

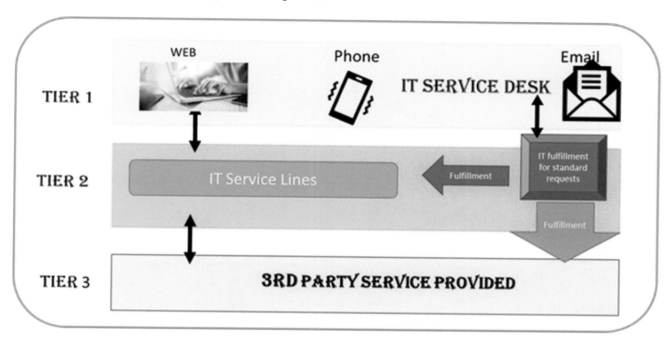

Figure 4:1:1 High Level Process Flow

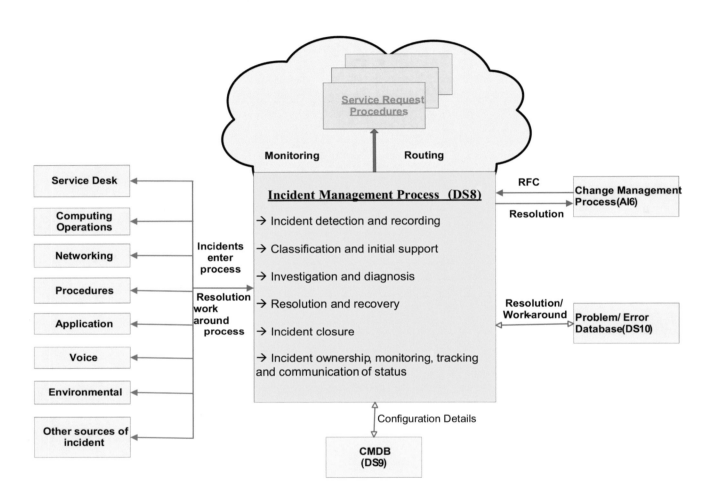

Figure 4:1:2 Incident Management Process Flow

DS8, DS9, DS10 and AI6 correspond to the COBIT®

5.2 Process Flow Overview

The Incident Management Process consists of the following activities:

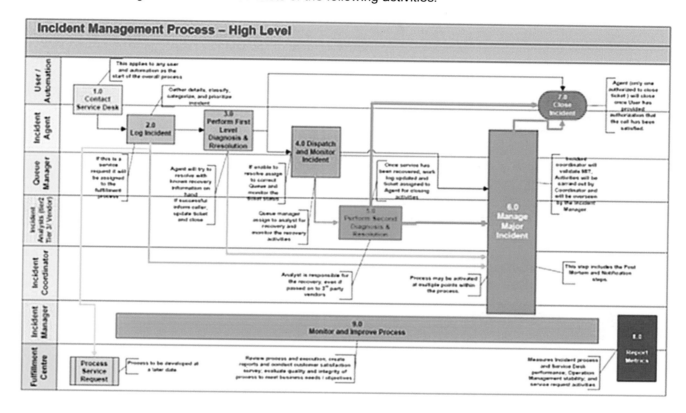

Figure 5:2.1 Incident Management Process

1.0 Contact Service Desk

This activity represents the starting point of the Incident Management process. Upon encountering a situation requiring ITS service support (i.e., service disruption or service request), the user will contact the Service desk via one of the authorized communication channels as defined by the contact codes. Section 7.2.

2.0 Log Incident

During this activity the information needed to create an incident record is collected. The key to this activity is the accurate and complete capture of user contact and incident description details. Based on the information collected, the Incident Agent classifies, categorizes, and prioritizes the incident.

If, during the initial logging, the incident symptoms reveal a potential Major Incident, the Incident Coordinator will be notified immediately for further validation and management.

The Incident may or may not represent a service impact. A Major incident may be called.

- If there is potential risk of affecting the reputation of Company ABXYZ
- Due to a major outage to a system impacting the organization significantly.
- For every security or privacy breach reported, which impacts the Confidentiality, Integrity, or availability of the production environment.

3.0 Perform First Level Diagnosis & Resolution

The Incident Agent will review the details, diagnose the situation, and identify the required course of action to resolve the incident as quickly as possible. The primary intent is to identify a prompt solution or workaround by reviewing previous incidents, leveraging knowledge repositories, reviewing known error / problem databases, or consulting with peers.

If the incident displays symptoms of a Major Incident, the Incident Coordinator will be notified immediately for further validation and management.

4.0 Dispatch and Monitor Incident

Following the investigation of the incident, if the Incident Agent is unable to identify a solution or workaround the incident is dispatched to a second level support group for further investigation.

If the Incident Agent is unclear which support group to dispatch the incident ticket to, the Incident Agent Lead Subject Matter Expert (SME) and / or Service Desk Team Lead will be consulted.

Following the dispatch of the Incident ticket, the Service Desk will continue to monitor the status of the incident and SLA / OLA adherence throughout the lifecycle.

5.0 Perform Second (nth) Level Diagnosis and Resolution

A thorough diagnosis is performed to find a workaround for service restoration. The assigned support group will review the details, perform an in-depth analysis of the incident symptoms, and formulate a solution or workaround to resolve the incident as quickly as possible. This team is fully accountable for the final resolution of the incident and has the authority to call upon other technical teams as required to ensure resolution time does not exceed service targets.

ITS Management team have agreed that Major Incident service recovery take precedence over all other activities.

If the incident displays symptoms of a Major Incident, the Incident Coordinator will be notified immediately for further validation and management.

6.0 Manage Major Incident

Upon being notified of a Major Incident, the Incident Coordinator will review the symptoms and validate the occurrence. Upon validation, the Incident Manager will oversee the technical resolution of the Major Incident and the appropriate MIT team assembled. The Incident Coordinator will then proceed to function as the primary communication point between the business and IT and oversee the Major Incident process execution.

7.0 Close Incident

Once the incident has been resolved and /or service has been delivered, the Service Desk will review the ticket for valid categorization and resolution data (work log activities and submission of Request for Change (RFC) as appropriate). The success of the resolution effort will be confirmed with the user prior to closing the incident ticket.

8.0 Report Metrics

This activity focuses on the generation and review of operational incident reports. These reports provide vital feedback on current Incident Management process and Service Desk performance, Operation Management stability, and service request activities.

9.0 Monitor and Improve Process

Routine reviews of the Incident Management process execution will be performed by the Incident Manager. Analysis of performance reports and customer satisfaction surveys will enable the Incident Manager to assess the quality and integrity of the process, verify alignment with business objectives, and minimize resource or ownership issues. If required, continuous improvement initiatives will be formulated to further refine and optimize the process.

Service Request Fulfillment

The Service Request Fulfillment external process contains activities that are specific to the lifecycle management of IT related Service Requests. Although the Incident Management process encompasses both IT Service Interruptions and Requests, unique supporting activities are required for enabling the order processing and fulfilling requirements associated with Service Requests.

1.0 Contact Service Desk	
Objective:	The purpose of this activity is for the end user to report an issue with any service deviations or a request for IT services (i.e., IT service deviation or service request) to the ITS Service Desk.
Roles:	The roles involved in the Contact Service Desk activity are: • User • Automation
Input:	The inputs to the Contact Service Desk activity are: • Identification of an IT service disruption or IT Service request requirement
Output:	The outputs of the Contact Service Desk activity are: • Notification of an IT service support request

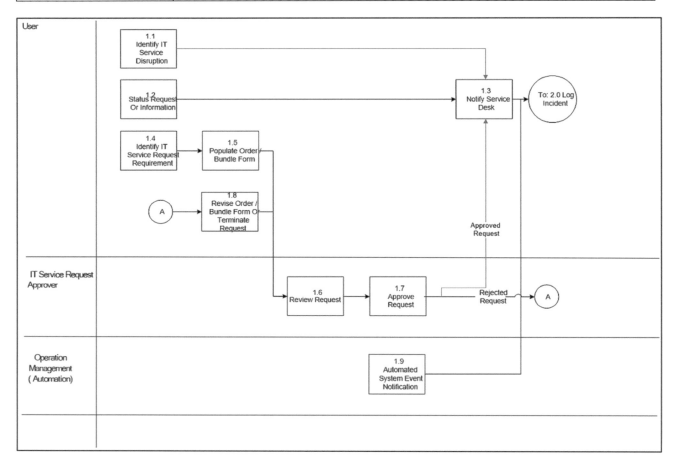

Figure 4:3:1 Contact Service Desk

Task: 1.1 Identify IT Service Disruption	**Role(s):** User

Tasks Description:
- Identification of a disruption to standard system operations / service delivery

Task: 1.2 Status Request	**Role(s):** User

Tasks Description:
- Submit a request inquiring about the resolution status of a previously logged Incident.

Task: 1.3 Notify Service Desk	**Role(s):** User

Tasks Description:
- Notify Service Desk of IT service support request.
  - Contact the Service Desk via one of the authorized communication channels:
    - Phone / Voicemail
    - E-Mail
    - Online
    - Web mail
    - Walk Up
      - (Note: This Walk-up communication channel is not formally endorsed by the Service Desk, although support will be provided should contact be made via this approach)

Task: 1.4 Identify Service Request Requirement	**Role(s):** User

Tasks Description:
- Identification of the need for an IT service request to improve or modify a user's IT usage capability.

Task: 1.5 Populate Order / Bundle Form	**Role(s):** User

Tasks Description:
- User to create the service request with all the details available to ensure no room for assumptions, to facilitate easy approval.

Task: 1.6 Review Request	**Role(s):** IT Service Request Approver

Tasks Description:
- Review request to ensure that the request is within the required guidelines of Software and Hardware requests. This should clearly define the recipient of the request.

Task: 1.7 Approve Request	**Role(s):** IT Service Request Approver

Tasks Description:
- Review request and provide approval or rejection.
- If rejected clearly identify reason for rejection. Proceed to next step 1.8 Revise Order / Bundle Form or Terminate Request
- If approved go to 1.3 Notify Service Desk

Task: 1.8 Revise Order / Bundle Form or Terminate Request	**Role(s):** User

Tasks Description:
- Review the rejected material and rework the request to address the identified reason for the rejection.

Task: 1.9 Automated System Event Notification	**Role(s):** Operation Management (Automation)

Tasks Description:
- Operation Management incident detected by event management tool.
- Notification issued to ITS Service Desk for automated incident ticket creation

2.0 Log Incident	
Objective:	The purpose of this activity is to receive and log the user's IT service support request. Upon receiving the request, the Incident Agent will determine whether the request pertains to a new incident or a status inquiry for a previously logged incident. For a new request, an incident ticket will be created, any relevant CIs associated, classification performed, and the severity defined based upon urgency and impact.
Roles:	The roles involved in the Log Incident activity are: • Incident Agent
Input:	The inputs to the Log Incident activity are: • Notification of an IT service support requirement
Output:	The outputs from the Log Incident activity are: • Logged and categorized incident ticket. And / Or • Service Request dispatched for fulfillment

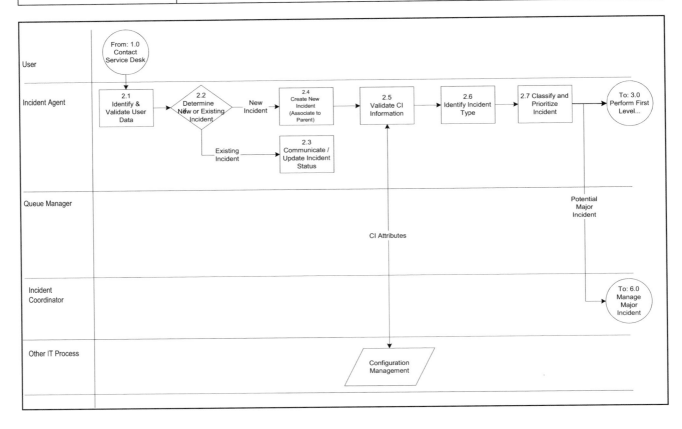

Figure 4:3:2 Log Incident

Task: 2.1 Identify & Validate User Data	**Role(s):** Incident Agent

Tasks Description:

- Receive user request.
- Identify user profile and validate for accuracy.
- Update or create user profile if applicable.
- Verify user entitlement for requested IT service.

Task: 2.2 Determine if New or Existing Incident	**Role(s):** Incident Agent

Tasks Description:

- Determine whether the request pertains to a new or previously logged incident.
  - If the request relates to a previously logged incident, proceed to 2.3 Communicate / Update Incident Status
  - If the request is for a new incident, proceed to 2.4 Create New Incident

Task: 2.3 Communicate / Update Incident Status	**Role(s):** Incident Agent

Tasks Description:

- Retrieve incident ticket.
- Advise user of incident status
- Update incident ticket with nature of status request
- If applicable, capture any additional user feedback which may aid in resolution efforts.

Task: 2.4 Create New Incident (Associate to Parent)	**Role(s):** Incident Agent

Tasks Description:

- Create incident ticket.
- Identify and document user incident details within ticket.
  - Review active incident Queue and determine if details align with a previously captured incident, if so, associate current incident to Parent Record ticket
    - **Parent Record** – A Parent record represents an incident where subsequent reporting of the same incident criteria is considered a repeat of the same underlying issue. Parent tickets are created when it is recognized that many calls may be received for the same service interruption. If the Parent Incident is resolved and the same issue recurs, a new Parent Incident will be generated for potential Childs to be associated to.
    - **Child Record** – A child record represents another user reporting the same service interruption as recorded in the parent, generally related to services having large customer base, i.e., network services, host services. Childs must have occurred during the duration of the Parent.

Task: 2.5 Validate Configuration Items (CI) Information	**Role(s):** Incident Agent

Tasks Description:

This practice is followed only in specific procedural instances. Will mature as CMDB develops.

- Check Configuration Items (CIs) connected to the caller and associate the specific CI about which he is calling to the incident ticket.
- Validate CI attribute accuracy with user.
  - If CI variance is encountered, update any inaccuracies, if possible, report discrepancy to Configuration Management manager, when the process is in place.

Task: 2.6 Identify Incident Type	**Role(s):** Incident Agent

Tasks Description:

- Review ticket details and determine if incident relates to an IT Service Disruption or Service Request

Task: 2.7 Classify and Prioritize Incident	**Role(s):** Incident Agent

Tasks Description:

- Review incident details and:
  - Classify ticket based on the respective Service and Component categories.
  - Define and Validate Severity Values
  - If incident is classified as a Severity 1 or 2, notify Incident Coordinator immediately to validate as a Major Incident. If major Incident, proceed to 6.0 Manage Major Incidents

3.0 Perform First Level Diagnosis & Resolution

Objective:	The purpose of this activity is to evaluate the incident symptoms and identify a quick solution or workaround. This is accomplished by reviewing previous incidents, leveraging knowledge repositories, reviewing known error / problem databases, or consulting with peers.
Roles:	The roles involved in the Perform First Level Diagnosis & Resolution activity are: • Incident Agent
Input:	The inputs to the Perform First Level Diagnosis & Resolution activity are: • Logged, classified, and prioritized incident ticket
Output:	The outputs from the Perform First Level Diagnosis & Resolution activity are: • Resolved incident. OR • Unresolved incident requiring dispatch to Tier-n support group. AND / OR • Incident Coordinator informed of a potential Major Incident

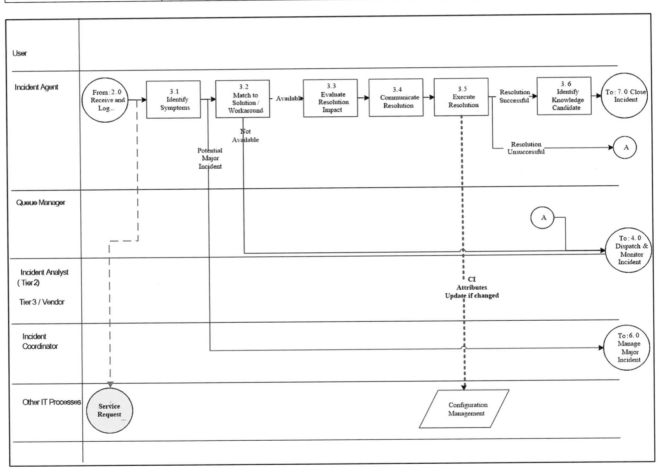

Figure 4:3:3 Perform First Level Diagnosis & Resolution

Task: 3.1 Identify Symptoms	**Role(s):** Incident Agent

Tasks Description:
- Review incident details and attempt to identify symptoms pertaining to affected Operation Management component or service.

If symptoms indicate a potential occurrence of a Major Incident, notify Incident Coordinator immediately to validate as a Major Incident. If Major incident, proceed to "6.0 Manage Major Incident"

Task: 3.2 Match to Solution / Workaround	**Role(s):** Incident Agent

Tasks Description:
- Match Incident with existing solution / workaround by searching incident repository, knowledge management system, reviewing known error / problem database, or consulting with peers.
  - If solution / workaround is available, proceed to "3.3 Evaluate Resolution Impact."
  OR
  - If solution / workaround is not available, proceed to "4.0 Dispatch and Monitor Incident"

Task: 3.3 Evaluate Resolution Impact	**Role(s):** Incident Agent

Tasks Description:
- Review Operation Management scope and potential impact of proposed resolution
- Evaluate resolution from both an IT and business operations perspective.

Task: 3.4 Communication Resolution	**Role(s):** Incident Agent

Tasks Description:
- Communicate scope and duration of proposed resolution effort to the user.
- Advise of any impacts or subsequent service disruptions
  - If applicable, communicate any interim workarounds to minimize impact of resolution efforts.

Task: 3.5 Execute Resolution	**Role(s):** Incident Agent

Tasks Description:
- Execute, together with the user, if necessary, the solution / workaround
- Perform internal validation of resolution execution success.
  - If resolution is unsuccessful, proceed to "4.0 Dispatch and Monitor Incident."
- Upon completion of resolution efforts, update any affected CIs, if applicable
- Document resolution details within Incident ticket (i.e., work log and resolution panels)
- Submit a Request for Change (RFC), as defined by the Change Management Process, if required based on the resolution activities.

Task: 3.6 Identify Knowledge Candidate	**Role(s):** Incident Agent

Tasks Description:
- Determine if the incident resolution is a unique solution / workaround that would be a suitable candidate for Knowledge Management
  - If true, nominate the solution / workaround to be considered by the Knowledge Management team (To make this a known error for future awareness and speedy recovery)

4.0 Dispatch and Monitor Incident	
Objective:	If a solution or workaround is not available, the incident is dispatched to a Tier-n support group for further investigation. Following the dispatch, the Service Desk will continue to monitor the incident ticket throughout its lifecycle to confirm status and gauge SLA / OLA adherence.
Roles:	The roles involved in the Dispatch and Monitor Incident activity are: • Incident Agent • Queue Manager • Incident Analyst
Input:	The inputs to the Dispatch and Monitor Incident activity are: • Unresolved incident
Output:	The outputs from Dispatch and Monitor Incident activity are: • Dispatched Incident to Tier-n support group AND / OR • Incident Coordinator informed of a potential Major Incident

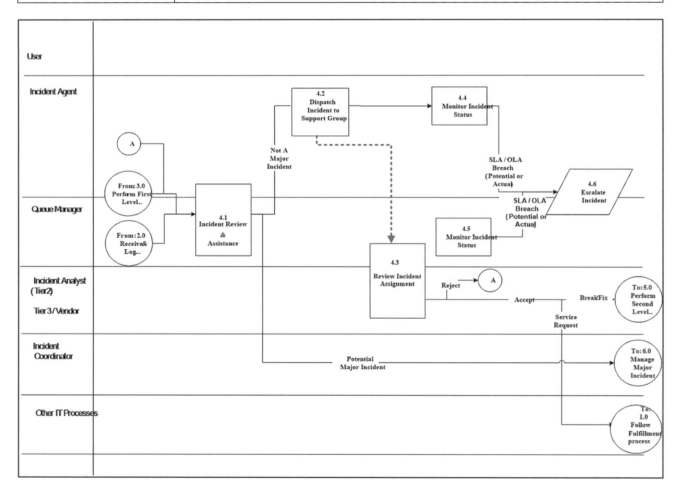

Figure 4:3:4 Dispatch and Monitor Incident

Task: 4.1 Incident Review & Assistance	**Role(s):** Queue Manager

Tasks Description:

- If the support group is unknown, consult with the respective Queue Manager for guidance on the appropriate support group to dispatch to

Task: 4.2 Dispatch Incident to Support Group	**Role(s):** Incident Agent

Tasks Description:

- Update incident ticket with:
  - Summary of investigation activities
  - Support group dispatch details
- Dispatch incident ticket to support group, as per reported issue.

Task: 4.3 Review Incident Assignment	**Role(s):** Queue Manager, Incident Analyst

Tasks Description:

- Review Incident ticket details to determine if target support group possesses the right skills to perform incident diagnosis:
  - If correctly assigned, accept the Incident ticket, and proceed to:
    - Service Issue - "5.0 Perform Second (nth) Level Diagnosis and Resolution"
    - Service Request – "1.0 Contact Service Order Desk"

    OR
  - If incorrectly assigned, update the work log with your reasons for reassignment and re-assign back to the Service Desk for correct dispatch. (If applicable, Queue Manager may attempt to re-classify the incident prior to re-assignment)

Task: 4.4 Monitor Incident Status	**Role(s):** Incident Agent

Tasks Description:

- Following the dispatch, the Service Desk continues to retain ownership of the incident ticket.
- To ensure optimal customer satisfaction and process adherence, continued monitoring of the incident throughout its lifecycle is performed.
- Monitoring includes:
  - Review support group resolution progress
  - Confirm incident ticket is being updated in a timely manner.
  - Monitor SLA / OLA adherence. Prior to and immediately following a breach engage support group to advise of service level adherence situation
  - Identify and initiate escalation activities.

Task: 4.5 Monitor Incident Status	**Role(s):** Queue Manager

Tasks Description:

- In tandem with the Incident Agent, the Queue Manager for the respective support Queue also monitors the incident throughout its lifecycle.
- This additional layer of monitoring ensures optimal resource and effort is applied towards incident resolution, process compliance, and reduced occurrences of service level disruptions due to inactivity.
- Monitoring includes:
  - Review support group resolution progress
  - Confirm incident ticket is being updated in a timely manner.
  - Monitor SLA / OLA adherence. Prior to and immediately following a breach engage support group to advise of service level adherence situation (Only applicable if Incident Agent was not able to perform this task).
  - Identify and initiate escalation activities

Task: 4.6 Escalate Incident	**Role(s):** Incident Agent, Queue Manager

Tasks Description:

- If a service level breach is anticipated or has occurred, escalation of the incident may be required.
- Refer to "Notification & Escalation Process" section for guidance.

5.0 Perform Second (nth) Level Diagnosis & Resolution	
Objective:	The purpose of this activity is to perform a more in-depth investigation since the initial analysis was not able to provide a solution / workaround. Throughout this activity, numerous subject matter experts may be consulted to formulate a resolution. If deeper analysis is required, the Problem Management process will manage.
Roles:	The roles involved in the Perform Second (nth) Level Diagnosis & Resolution activity are: • Incident Analyst • Tier 3 / Vendor
Input:	The inputs to the Perform Second (nth) Level Diagnosis & Resolution activity are: • Unresolved incident
Output:	The outputs from Perform Second (nth) Level Diagnosis & Resolution activity are: • Resolved incident. AND / OR • Incident Coordinator informed of a potential Major Incident for consideration.

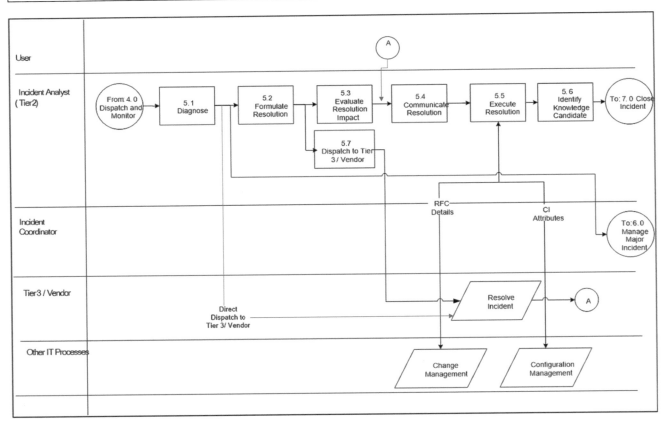

Figure 4:3:5 Perform Second (nth) Level Diagnosis & Resolution

Task: 5.1 Diagnose	**Role(s):** Incident Analyst

Tasks Description:
- Review resolution activities performed by Incident Agent
  - If all steps/information defined within the knowledge base record were not carried out effectively by the Incident Agent, update the work log with your reasons for reassignment and reassign the ticket back to the Service Desk taking appropriate action to ensure SLA is not breached.
- Perform in-depth analysis of incident symptoms.
- Consult with user on incident symptoms, if required
- Consult with other IT support groups and external vendors, if applicable
- Formulate incident diagnosis.
  - If diagnosis reveals Major Incident symptoms, notify the Incident Coordinator for further analysis. Proceed to "6.0 Manage Major Incident".
  - If diagnosis reveals that the failing component is not as originally diagnosed by the Service Desk, update the Component Category, document your diagnosis and recommendations in the ticket and reassign the ticket back to the Service Desk

Task: 5.2 Formulate Resolution	**Role(s):** Incident Analyst

Tasks Description:
- Review incident diagnosis summary and formulate incident solution / workaround.
  - If a resolution can be formulated, proceed to "5.3 Evaluate Resolution Impact."
    OR
  - If a resolution can is not formulated:
    - Dispatch incident to Tier 3 / Vendor for deeper investigation. Proceed to the "5.7 Dispatch to Tier 3 / Vendor"

Task: 5.3 Evaluate Resolution Impact	**Role(s):** Incident Analyst

Tasks Description:
- Review Operation Management scope and potential impact of proposed resolution
- Evaluate resolution from both an IT and business operations perspective.

Task: 5.4 Communication Resolution	**Role(s):** Incident Analyst

Tasks Description:
- Communicate scope and duration of proposed resolution effort to the user.
- Advise of any impacts or subsequent service disruptions
  - If applicable, communicate any interim workarounds to minimize impact of resolution efforts.

Task: 5.5 Execute Resolution	**Role(s):** Incident Analyst

Tasks Description:
- Execute, together with the user, if necessary, the solution / workaround OR validate Tier 3 / Vendor resolution details
- If the resolution plan involves a change, the Change Management process is initiated.
- Perform internal validation of resolution execution success.
- Update Closure Component Category to reflect the actual failing components that was corrected to restore normal services. Update the Closure Service Component Category to identify the service that the component is provided by.
- Update the work log, Closure Codes and Closure Resolution fields to provide accurate synopsis of incident diagnosis and resolution actions performed to restore service.
- If you were in contact with the end user and have confirmed directly that the service was restored, indicate so in the work log.

Task: 5.6 Identify Knowledge Candidate	**Role(s):** Incident Analyst

Tasks Description:
- Determine if the incident resolution is a unique solution / workaround that would be a suitable candidate for Knowledge Management
  - If true, nominate the solution / workaround to be considered by the Knowledge Management team.

Task: 5.7 Dispatch to Tier 3 / Vendor	**Role(s):** Incident Analyst

Tasks Description:
- Document unsuccessful resolution effort and dispatch incident to Tier 3 / Vendor
- Ticket will be left as 'In Progress'
- When a resolution is arrived at by Tier 3, go to '5.3 evaluate resolution impact'.

6.0 Manage Major Incidents	
Objective:	The purpose of this activity is to facilitate the prompt recovery of IT services following a severe disruption or extreme impact. This is accomplished by providing accurate identification and validation of Major Incidents, concise and timely notification, optimal resource assignments and recovery plans, and comprehensive postmortem activities. A Major Incident is a significant IT event leading to a severe impact to IT service delivery, or where the disruption is deemed unacceptably excessive, as defined in SLAs. The Incident may or may not represent a service impact. A Major incident may be called.<ul><li>If there is potential risk of affecting the reputation of Company ABXYZ</li><li>Due to a major outage to a system impacting the organization significantly.</li><li>For every security or privacy breach reported, which impacts the Confidentiality, Integrity, or availability of the production environment.</li></ul>**Note:** *This document does not include standards and procedures for Disaster Recovery and Business Continuity situations. The Computer Emergency Response Team (CERT) Manage these under their defined process.*
Roles:	The roles involved in the Manage Major Incidents activity are:<ul><li>Incident Coordinator</li><li>**Major Incident Team (Representative from IT Service Lines Groups, including Security)**</li><li>Incident Manager</li><li>Incident Agent</li></ul>
Input:	The inputs to the Manage Major Incidents activity are:<ul><li>One or more unresolved incidents identified as a potential Major Incident</li></ul>
Output:	The outputs from Manage Major Incidents activity are:<ul><li>Resolved Major Incident</li></ul>

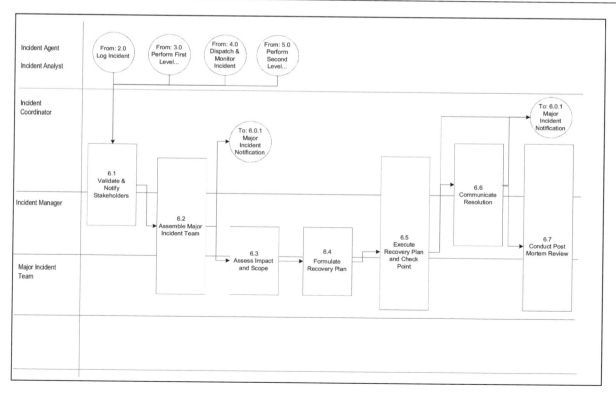

Figure 4:3:6 Manage Major Incident

Task: 6.1 Validate and Notify Stakeholders	**Role(s):** Incident Coordinator, Incident Manager

Tasks Description:
- Review and validate potential Major Incident
  - Assess incident symptoms against Major Incident Classification Criteria
  - Reviewing findings with Incident Manager
- Upon validation of the Major Incident, update the Incident ticket to Severity 1
- Distribute Major Incident Notifications to recipients (*refer to Major Incident Notifications 6.0.1*)

Task: 6.2 Assemble Major Incident Team	**Role(s):** Incident Coordinator (IC), Incident Manager (IM), Major Incident Team (MIT)

Tasks Description:
- Incident Manager notifies, assembles, and coordinates Major Incident Team, based upon the complexity of the situation. All meeting objectives defined below may be accomplished without a formal meeting but must be addressed by the Incident Manager.
  - MIT members will respond within **15 minutes** to any MIT invitation page by calling the Conference Bridge line.
    - Local line is: _____
    - 800 line is: _____
    - Moderator id is: _____ followed by # key.
    - Participants id is _____ followed by # Key.
- Conduct Major Incident Review Meeting
  - Meeting objectives:
  - Review scope of Major Incident (IC)
  - Incident Manager formally identified as the individual responsible for managing the technical aspect of the recovery effort (IC)
  - Initiate diagnosis tasks to identify the probable cause of the incident (MIT)
  - Ensure appropriate resources have been acquired to work on investigation and resolution activities (IM)
  - Initiate business impact mitigation analysis to identify potential workarounds for temporarily restoring business functions to the customer. (MIT).
    - If applicable:
      - Develop action plan for the coordination and execution of business impact mitigation efforts (IC, MIT)
      - Determine and acquire the appropriate resources (IC)

Task: 6.3 Assess Impact and Scope	**Role(s):** Major Incident Team, Incident Manager, Incident Coordinator

Tasks Description:
- Assess Major Incident Impact and Scope from a business and technical perspective (MIT, IM)
- Determine resolution resource logistics and timeframe (IM)
- Identify potential business impacts (i.e., user disruptive on-site activities to be performed) (MIT, IM)
  - If business impact is confirmed, notify Incident Coordinator
  - Incident Coordinator facilitates communication between appropriate teams (i.e., external support groups, vendors, business stakeholders, etc.) to establish action plan for addressing and mitigating external impacts

Task: 6.4 Formulate Recovery Plan	**Role(s):** Incident Manager, Major Incident Team

Tasks Description:

- Establish recovery plan consisting of:
    - Detailed breakdown of the recovery activities and any associated changes
    - Resource requirements
    - Anticipated timeframe
    - Back-out plan
    - Test plan
    - Communication plan
    - Post implementation monitoring activities.
- Analyze the incident, the full impact of the action(s) to be taken and balance the risk of premature action versus the need to restore the service (MIT).
- All decisions and actions are subject to the agreement of the MIT (Technical and Business participants).
- If the recovery activities involve a change or service interruption, the Change Management process is initiated (the Change Manager may be part of the MIT Group)
- Review the recovery plan with the appropriate parties and stakeholders to ensure the impact of the resolution activities are acceptable.
    - Recommended parties:
        - Incident Coordinator
        - Incident Manager
        - Change Management Team
        - Business Stakeholders / Service Provider(s) (if required)
        - *Note: Appropriate parties may vary based on nature of incident*

Task: 6.5 Execute Recovery Plan and Check Point	**Role(s):** Major Incident Team, Incident Manager, Incident Coordinator

Tasks Description:

- Execute recovery plan.
- Provide intermittent status updates to Incident Coordinator (as defined within recovery plan)
    - If the resolution effort is being performed by an internal support group or a 3rd party vendor, status updates will be issued directly to the Queue Manager, who in turn will review with the Incident Manager and then with the Incident Coordinator.
    - If a significant situation should arise prior to the next periodic status update, inform the Incident Coordinator of the situation immediately.
- Incident Coordinator reviews updates and monitors recovery progress:
    - If resolution efforts are not progressing according to plan or escalation conditions are met, invoke escalation activities (*Refer to "4.4 Notification and Escalation Process"*)
    - If a significant change in resolution progress is observed, distribute Major Incident notification updates to recipients (*refer to "6.0.1 Major Incident Notifications"*)
- Upon completion of the recovery plan, Major Incident team confirms resolution satisfaction with user.
    - If the customer is unsatisfied with the resolution, further investigation / escalation is required.

Task: 6.6 Communicate Resolution	**Role(s):** Incident Coordinator, Incident Manager, Major Incident Team

Tasks Description:
- Incident Manager reviews resolution details
  - o Confirm all activities defined within the recovery plan have been achieved.
  - o Verify that the client has confirmed their satisfaction with the resolution.
- Update incident ticket to resolved state.
- Notify Incident Coordinator of resolution.
- Incident Coordinator verifies resolution chronology has been documented within incident ticket.
- Distribute Major Incident notifications to recipients advising of resolved status (*refer to "6.0.1 Major Incident Notifications"*)
- The scribe (Incident Coordinator) will ensure that the incident record contains the following:
  - Incident description
  - chronology/incident details
  - recovery steps
  - results
  - duration of service impact (partial or full)
  - MIT required = yes
  - service impact = yes or no (pro-active recovery)
  - service impact (description)
  - MIT minutes (i.e. MIT actions, etc.)
  - the MIT start time
  - the MIT end time
  - the MIT Facilitator name
  - the MIT members
  - incident to problem transition (If recovery is associated with a recurring incident or failure following the recovery of the service)
- Record key points and hi-lights.
- At logical break points scribe will update with activities/chronology.
- Assign ticket to Incident Agent for closing.

Task: 6.7 Conduct Postmortem Review	**Role(s):** Management, Incident Manager, Incident Coordinator, Customer Service, Major Incident Team, Responsible Manager

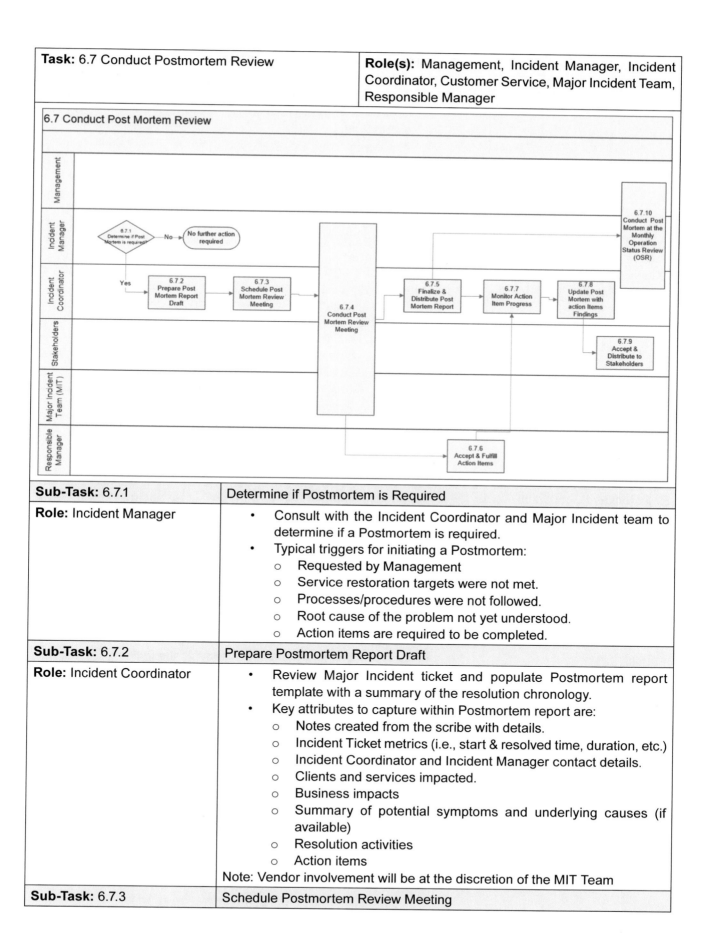

Sub-Task: 6.7.1	Determine if Postmortem is Required
Role: Incident Manager	<ul><li>Consult with the Incident Coordinator and Major Incident team to determine if a Postmortem is required.</li><li>Typical triggers for initiating a Postmortem:<ul><li>Requested by Management</li><li>Service restoration targets were not met.</li><li>Processes/procedures were not followed.</li><li>Root cause of the problem not yet understood.</li><li>Action items are required to be completed.</li></ul></li></ul>
Sub-Task: 6.7.2	Prepare Postmortem Report Draft
Role: Incident Coordinator	<ul><li>Review Major Incident ticket and populate Postmortem report template with a summary of the resolution chronology.</li><li>Key attributes to capture within Postmortem report are:<ul><li>Notes created from the scribe with details.</li><li>Incident Ticket metrics (i.e., start & resolved time, duration, etc.)</li><li>Incident Coordinator and Incident Manager contact details.</li><li>Clients and services impacted.</li><li>Business impacts</li><li>Summary of potential symptoms and underlying causes (if available)</li><li>Resolution activities</li><li>Action items</li></ul></li></ul>Note: Vendor involvement will be at the discretion of the MIT Team
Sub-Task: 6.7.3	Schedule Postmortem Review Meeting

Role: Incident Coordinator	• Schedule Postmortem review meeting with Major Incident team and required stakeholders.
	o To ensure improved business impact analysis and action item accountability, advise ITS Operation resource meeting occurrence.
	o Include Postmortem draft and Incident ticket within meeting invite.
	• Meeting attendance is mandatory, if a resource is unable to attend, a delegate, who participated in or has knowledge of the Major Incident must be identified to attend in his/her place.
Sub-Task: 6.7.4	Conduct Postmortem Review Meeting
Role: Incident Manager, Incident Coordinator, Customer Service, Major Incident Team	• Incident Manager will facilitate the Postmortem Review Meeting
	• Purpose of the meeting is to review and establish consensus on Postmortem report content and identify follow-on action items.
	o Incident Coordinator will walkthrough the details of the incident work log, resolution text, and the draft Postmortem report
	• Based on the findings and recommendations raised during the meeting, document a list of action items within the *"Major Incident Action Items Tracking Log (Appendices 10.2.2)"*
	o Action items may encompass Investigation Reports, Detail Analysis Report, follow-on resolution activities, and / or Root Cause Analysis (RCA) activities (RCA will be removed from Incident Management Postmortem scope upon formalization of the ITS Problem Management process)
Sub-Task: 6.7.5	Finalize & Distribute Postmortem Report
Role: Incident Coordinator	• Update and finalize Postmortem report based on feedback from the Postmortem Review meeting.
	• Distribute Postmortem report to review meeting attendees (i.e., Major Incident team and stakeholders)
Sub-Task: 6.7.6	Accept & Fulfill Action Items
Role: Responsible Manager	• Review the Action Item(s) and determine if the content is applicable to the operation support group's focus area.
	• If applicable, acknowledge the acceptance of the action item and provide an estimated completion date.
	• If not applicable, return the action items to the Incident Coordinator for reassignment.
	• Review details of the action item and assign to the appropriate resource within the support group.
	• Once assigned, monitor the progress of the action item to ensure it is completed by the due date specified.
Sub-Task: 6.7.7	Monitor Action Item Progress
Role: Incident Coordinator	• At predefined intervals (i.e., weekly) follow-up with action item assignees on the status of fulfillment activities
	• Monitor adherence to target completion date, if a failure to complete on time is anticipated engage assigned resources to determine if escalation activities are required.
	• Note: Incident Coordinator is responsible for monitoring the status of open action items. If escalation is required, the Incident Manager is accountable for managing the escalation activities.
Sub-Task: 6.7.8	Update Postmortem Report with Action Item Findings

Role: Incident Coordinator	• Upon completion of each assigned action item, update the Postmortem report with the respective findings. • If the findings introduce a significant change to the Postmortem content, re-distribute an updated version of the Postmortem report.
Sub-Task: 6.7.9	(IF APPLICABLE) Accept & Distribute to Customer
Role: Customer Service	• Receive Postmortem report and review content to ensure details align with customer request requirements (i.e., assurance applied resolution activities will prevent future reoccurrences) • Distribute Postmortem report to designated customer recipients.
Sub-Task: 6.7.10	Conduct Postmortem at the Monthly Operation Status Review (OSR)
Role: Management, Incident Manager, Incident Coordinator	• Schedule monthly review meeting with ITS Management • Provide a summary of the completed Postmortem Reports • Identify any Postmortem Reports with outstanding action items. Initiate escalation activities if required.

6.0.1 Major Incident Notifications

Objective:	The purpose of this activity is to notify and periodically update stakeholders of the declared Major Incident.
Roles:	The roles involved in the Major Incident Notification activity are: • Incident Coordinator • Incident Manager • Incident Agent
Input:	The inputs to the Major Incident Notification activity are: • Major Incident identified. • Major Incident status updates • Major Incident resolved
Output:	The outputs of the Major Incident Notification activity are: • Management Notification (Approved Messaging) • IVR Greeting Message (Phones) • Briefing Note • Client Communication

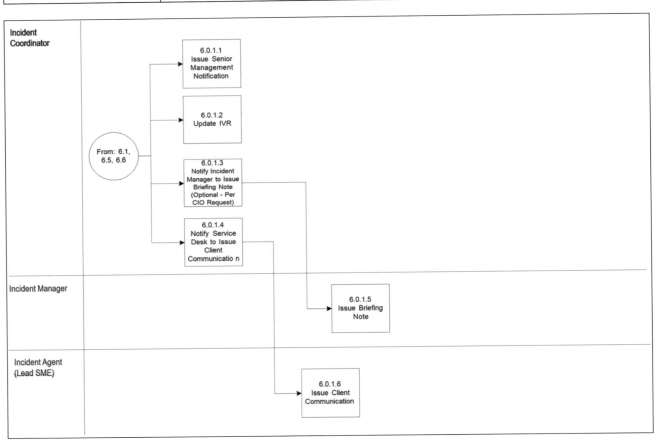

Note:
Refer to section "4.4 Notification and Escalation Process" for guidance on notification type frequency target recipients, and structure.

Task: 6.0.1.1 Issue Management Notification	**Role(s):** Incident Coordinator

Tasks Description:
- Advise Management of Major Incident occurrence by notifying the recipients defined within approved Messaging distribution list.
    - Note: Based on the nature of the Major Incident, the default recipient list may need to be modified

Task: 6.0.1.2 Update IVR	**Role(s):** Incident Coordinator

Tasks Description:
- Update the Service Desk IVR greeting message with details pertaining to the Major Incident
- Refer to Appendix 10.3.2 for Service Desk IVR Broadcast

Task: 6.0.1.3 Notify Incident Manager to Issue Briefing Note (Optional - Per CIO Request)	**Role(s):** Incident Coordinator, Incident Manager

Tasks Description:
- If requested by CIO, notify the Incident Manager to issue an Executive Briefing Note

Task: 6.0.1.4 Notify Service Desk to Issue Client Communication	**Role(s):** Incident Coordinator, Incident Manager, Incident Agent

Tasks Description:
- Incident Coordinator and Incident Manager agree on content of Client Communication
- Incident Agent generates and distributes the Client Communication outlining the scope and impact associated with the Major Incident

Task: 6.0.1.5 Issue Briefing Note	**Role(s):** Incident Manager

Tasks Description:
- Review Major Incident details and align with briefing note template requirements.
    - If additional details are required, consult with the Incident Coordinator
- Upon completion of the briefing note, obtain sign-off from ITS Management and forward to the respective business executives.
- Refer to Appendix 10.3.3 and 10.3.4 for Executive Briefing Note sample.

Task: 6.0.1.6 Issue Client Communication	**Role(s):** Incident Agent

Tasks Description:
- Review Major Incident ticket and consult with Incident Coordinator to determine latest status of the Major Incident
- Document Major Incident Client Communication and distribute to impacted clients.
- Refer to Appendix 10.3 for Client Communication sample.

7.0 Close Incident	
Objective:	The purpose of this activity is to validate the incident resolution effort with the user and gauge their satisfaction level prior to incident ticket closure.
Roles:	The roles involved in Close Incident activity are: • Incident Agent
Input:	The inputs to Close Incident activity are: • Resolved incident
Output:	The outputs from Close Incident activity are: • Closed incident ticket (break / fix) or resolved Service Request • Knowledge Database Submission (if applicable)

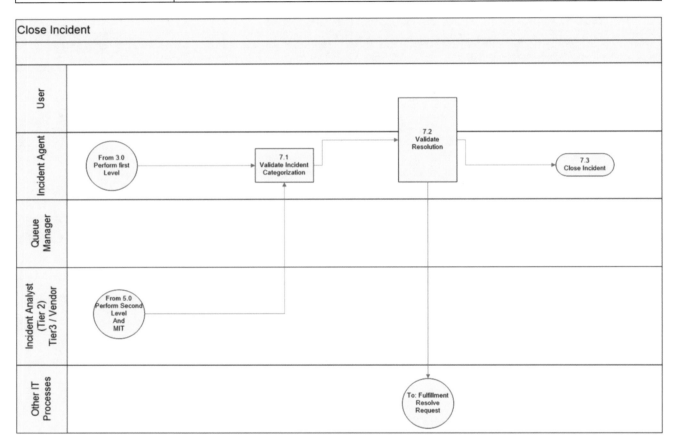

Figure 4:3:7 Close Incident

Task: 7.1 Validate Incident Categorization	**Role(s):** Incident Agent

Tasks Description:
- Verify the incident record for completion and content accuracy. If incomplete, contact operation support areas, user, etc. for missing information required to complete record.
- While resolving this incident, it may be determined that the initial categorization values captured in the Component/Service Category field (Details tab) do not represent the actual failing component or service.
- Based on the incident resolution information, update the current Component and Category field (resolution tab) with the correct categorization values, if you did not resolve the incident, confirm with the resolver prior to changing these values.

Task: 7.2 Validate Resolution	**Role(s):** Incident Agent

Tasks Description:
- Review incident resolution effort with user
- Validate resolution success with user.
- Obtain user confirmation that IT service disruption has been resolved.
  - If user is not satisfied with resolution, dispatch the incident to the Service Desk Team Lead / Queue Manager for escalation confirmation and guidance.
  - Refer to "4.4 Notification & Escalation Process" for guidance on hierarchical escalations.
- If Incident relates to a Service Request, follow the established closing criteria as per the fulfillment process.

Task: 7.3 Close Incident	**Role(s):** Incident Agent

Tasks Description:
- Close incident ticket within the Service Management tool

8.0 Report Metrics	
Objective:	The purpose of this activity is to define metrics and generate reports related to incident management operational activities These reports provide vital feedback on service level adherence, current Incident Management process and Service Desk performance, Operation Management stability, and Service Request activities.
Roles:	The roles involved in Report Metrics Process activity are: • Incident Coordinator • Incident Manager • Incident Management Process Owner • Process Stakeholders
Input:	The inputs to the Report Metrics activity are: • Incident Management Reporting Request / Requirements
Output:	The outputs from the Report Metrics activity are: • Incident Management Reports

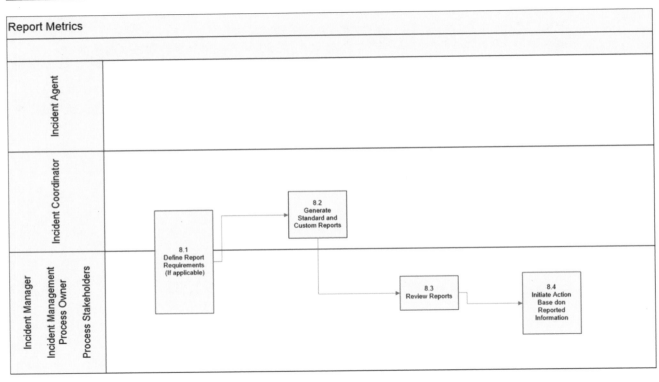

Figure 4:3:8 Report Metrics

Task: 8.1 Define Report Requirements	**Role(s):** Incident Coordinator, Incident Manager, Incident Management Process Owner, Process Stakeholders

Tasks Description:
- Establish Incident Management reporting requirements.
- Potential Triggers:
  - New Service Activation
  - Service Provider / Stakeholder Request
  - SLA / OLA failure to meet agreed to targets.
  - Postmortem Action Item (via the Monthly Operation Status Review)
  - Continuous Improvement Initiative (as identified by the MIT, Leads or Management)

Task: 8.2 Generate Standard and Custom Reports	**Role(s):** Incident Coordinator

Tasks Description:
- Based on the defined reporting schedule, generate standard and custom reports
- If required, distribute reports to defined recipients and stakeholders.

Task: 8.3 Review Reports	**Role(s):** Incident Manager, Incident Management Process Owner, Process Stakeholders

Tasks Description:
- Acquire reports and review based on adherence to defined Service Level / performance targets on an agreed schedule.

Task: 8.4 Initiate Action Based on Reported Information	**Role(s):** Incident Manager, Incident Management Process Owner, Process Stakeholders

Tasks Description:
- Based on findings from reports, formulate and initiate actions (if applicable)
- Potential actions:
  - Service Level modifications (to be negotiated as part of regular Service Review meeting)
  - Service Improvement Program
  - Incident Management process improvement
  - Service Desk function or technology improvement
  - Operation Management changes
  - Incident trending and problem investigation
- For wider visibility and awareness elevate the metrics to CobiT ME4

9.0 Monitor and Improve Process	
Objective:	The purpose of this activity is to perform routine evaluations of the Incident Management process performance and component relevancy. The intent is to identify process improvement opportunities to further enhance the effectiveness and efficiency of the ITS Incident Management process.
Roles:	The roles involved in Monitor and Improve Process activity are: • Incident Manager • Incident Management Process Owner
Input:	The inputs to Monitor and Improve Process activity are: • Process Reports • Customer Survey Feedback • Service Desk / Operation Support Group Feedback
Output:	The outputs from Monitor and Improve Process activity are: • Process Improvement Initiative

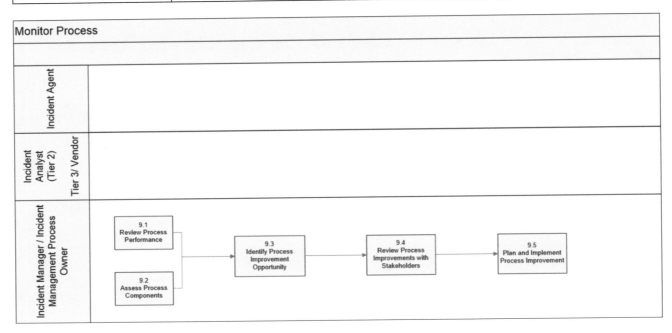

Figure 4:3:9 Monitor Process

Task: 9.1 Review Process Performance	Role(s): Incident Manager/ Process Owner

Tasks Description:

- Review Incident Management process performance by:
  - Evaluating process performance and trending reports
  - Analyzing Customer Satisfaction survey results
  - Assessing Incident Agent and Operation Support Group Incident handling feedback
- Compare findings against predefined service level agreements (SLAs or OLAs)

Task: 9.2 Assess Process Components	Role(s): Incident Manager/ Process Owner

Tasks Description:

- On a regular basis, assess the process components defined with the Incident Management Process Guide
  - Note: During the initial implementation or following a major improvement, assess process components on a 3-month basis, during steady state, yearly assessments should be performed.
- Process components should be assessed to confirm alignment with current business objectives, organizational structure, technology implications, and capability to attain service level commitments.
- Specific process components which should be assessed are:
  - Process Foundations
  - Process activities and supporting tasks.
  - Process integration with other IT process
  - Roles & Responsibilities
  - Policies
  - Measurements and reporting capabilities.
  - Technology enablement
  - Quality Control process

Task: 9.3 Identify Process Improvement Opportunity	Role(s): Incident Manager/ Process Owner

Tasks Description:

- Based on input from Process Performance and / or Component review, identify process execution gaps or opportunities to refine / optimize process effectiveness and efficiency
- Formulate plan to address opportunity.
- Identify stakeholders who may be impacted by improvement initiative.

Task: 9.4 Review Process Improvement with Stakeholders	Role(s): Incident Manager/ Process Owner

Tasks Description:

- Review process improvement action plan with stakeholders
- Assess impact of improvement from both an IT and business perspective
  - Determine the effect upon the Operation Management and customer service, as defined by service level agreements, and upon Operation Management capacity and performance, reliability and resilience, contingency plans, and security

Task: 9.5 Plan & Implement Process Improvement	Role(s): Incident Manager/ Process Owner

Tasks Description:

- Formulate implementation plan for process improvement initiative.
- If Operation Management change is required, submit RFC to interface with Change Management
- If required:
  - Establish communication plan to communicate upcoming process improvement.
  - Develop training plan for both operation support personnel and users.
  - Interface with Service Level Management to revise applicable SLAs and OLAs
- Monitor implementation efforts to ensure results align with objectives.
- Update the Process Guide once the recommendations have been updated

5.3 Notification and Escalation Process

A key enabler for enforcing and achieving service level requirements is accomplished via the timely execution of notification and escalation activities. The following directive, process and procedures provide a comprehensive outline of the activities contained within the Incident Management process for initiating and managing escalation situations.

5.3.1 Notification Types

Depending on the incident severity, varying types of incident notifications will be generated. The primary objectives are to:

- Ensure operation support groups are aware that an incident ticket has been assigned to their Queue.
- Ensure all appropriate users, operation support staff, and stakeholders are aware of the incident identification.
- Provide up to date information regarding incident status to those users / operation support staff / and stakeholders who wish to be kept informed.
- Ensure appropriate escalations are followed for High Severity incidents.

This type will only apply to the committed hours of service.

Notification Type	Description	Severity Applicability	Frequency	Preferred Method	Recipients
Assignment Notification	Automated notification advising the appropriate operation support group that an incident has been assigned to their Queue.	All Severity Levels	Upon assignment to an operation support Queue	Automated E-Mail	To: Queue manager, Operation support Group Agent / Analysts
Incident Ticket Status Notifications	Automated notification advising of a change in the status of the incident ticket at pre-defined intervals.	All Severity Levels	Incident Ticket Status = Assigned, Pending, Resolved / Fulfilled	Automated E-Mail	To: User associated to incident ticket
Client Communication	Advises all affected clients of incident occurrence and status of on-going resolution efforts	Sev 1 & 2	**Identification:** <= 15 min	E-Mail from Incident Coordinator	To: Business Unit
		Sev 1	**On-going Resolution:** Business Hours Every 3 hours or as status changes After Hours As status changes		CC: ITS Service Desk, Incident Manager
		Sev 2	As status changes		
			Final Resolution: <= 15 min		
Approved Messaging	Provides CIO Office and management team with prompt notification of Major Incident occurrence and status of on-going resolution efforts.	Sev 1 & 2	**Identification:** <= 15 min	E-Mail from Incident Coordinator	To: CIO Office, ITS Management, Incident Manager, Internal Business Contacts
		Sev 1	**On-going Resolution:** Business Hours Every 3 hours or as status changes After Hours As status changes		
		Sev 2	As status changes		
			Final Resolution: <= 15 min		

Notification Type	Description	Severity Applicability	Frequency	Preferred Method	Recipients
Briefing Note	Ensures CIO office is made aware of Major Incident occurrence and on-going resolution efforts	Sev 1 *(Optional based on either CIO office request or trigger criteria – refer to "Frequency" column)*	**Identification:** <u>Within 1 to 2 hours:</u> - Outage > 4 business hrs. - Incident affecting sensitive system or environment - Virus Outbreak <u>Within 30 minutes:</u> - CIO's Office Request **On-going Resolution:** Daily updates **Final Resolution:** Within 2 to 4 hours of resolution	E-Mail from Incident Manager	To: CIO Office. ITS Management CC: As requested by affected CIO
IVR Broadcast	Inform all callers to the ITS Service Desk of the occurrence and resolution of a Major Incident	Sev 1 Sev 2 (Optional based upon # of impacted users)	**Identification:** <= 15 min **On-going Resolution:** <u>Business Hours</u> Every 3 hours or as status changes <u>After Hours</u> As status changes **Final Resolution:** <= 15 min	IVR Broadcast recorded by Incident Coordinator	To: Service Desk Clients
Potential Major Incident	Automated notification advising the Incident Coordinator that a Major Incident is to be validated	Sev 1 & 2	Upon creation of a Severity 1 or 2 incident	Automated E-Mail from tool	To: Incident Coordinators Incident Managers

Identification of the specific persons to notify will be based upon the Service Affected. This information is communicated, by the ITS operation support group, to the Service Desk and must be always current to ensure accuracy.

5.3.2 Escalation Protocol

The objective of the Escalation is to ensure that the appropriate resources are assigned to provide an incident with the required attention to achieve a resolution.

Incident escalations are typically invoked via:

- **Service Level Escalation:** Resolution efforts are not progressing according to plan or service level 'not in compliance' has occurred. Service level escalations may result in acquisition of additional operation support resources (internal or 3rd party) or initiation of stakeholder communications.
- **Hierarchical Escalation:** User is not satisfied with the current service being attained and therefore requests an escalation be invoked to address their concerns. Upon receiving an escalation request, the Incident Agent validates the request with the Service Desk Team Lead. Upon validation of the escalation request, initiation of the escalation hierarchy is commenced. Alternatively, hierarchical escalations can be initiated internally by operation support staff, Stakeholders, Management to address Incident Management process exceptions or issues with resolution efforts.

To invoke an escalation, the escalation initiator (i.e., Incident Agent or Analyst) will provide the escalation recipients with the following information:

- **Issue**: Brief synopsis of the scope and impact of the incident
- **Current Status**: Summary of the current state of the incident and the resolution efforts performed to date.
- **Escalation Trigger:** Reason for invoking the escalation directive and summary of any previous escalation efforts.
- **Next Escalation Trigger**: Information about how and when the next escalation will be triggered.
- **NOTE:** % SLA refers to the % of elapsed time for the committed service recovery.

5.3.3 Escalation Guidelines

Priority	SLA / OLA Triggers	Severity 1 Contact	Severity 2 Contact	Severity 3 Contact	Severity 4 Contact
4	25% SLA / OLA	Incident Manager	N/A	N/A	N/A
3	50% SLA / OLA	Team Leads	Incident Manager	Queue Manager	Queue Manager
2	75% SLA / OLA	Management	Team Leads	Queue Manager / Team Leads	Queue Manager / Team Leads
1	SLA / OLA Not in compliance	CIO	Management	Team Lead	Team Lead

Priority	Hierarchical Escalation	Severity 1	Severity 2	Severity 3	Severity 4
4	1st Escalation	Incident Manager 0 - 30 minutes	Incident Manager 0 - 60 minutes	Team Lead 0 - 4 hours	Team Lead 0 -1 day
3	2nd Escalation	Team Leads 31 – 60 minutes	Team Leads 1 – 2 hours	N/A	N/A
2	3rd Escalation	Management 61 – 90 minutes	Management 2 – 3 hours	N/A	N/A
1	Final Escalation	CIO Over 90 minutes	N/A	N/A	N/A

Severity Notification & Escalation

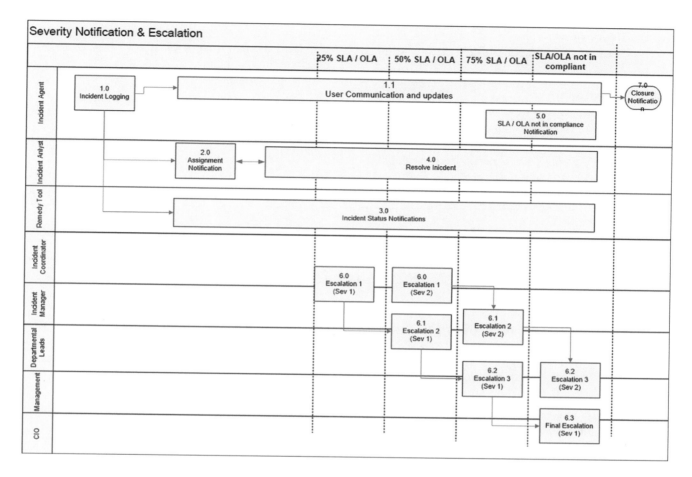

5.3.4 Severity Notification & Escalation Process

Task: 1.0 Incident Logging	Role(s): Incident Agent
Tasks Description: • User contacts the Service Desk to request IT operation support or IT fulfillment services. • Incident Agent logs and classifies incident ticket with relevant details. • If required dispatch to Incident Analyst for in-depth diagnosis and resolution activities	
Task: 1.1 User Communication and Updates	Role(s): Incident Agent
Tasks Description: • Proactively keep all affected users advised of incident status. • Respond to user inquiries regarding incident status. • Receive and manage user initiated incident escalation requests.	
Task: 2.0 Assignment Notification	Role(s): tool, Incident Analyst
Tasks Description: • Automated Assignment Notification advising the receiving operation support group of an incident assigned to their Queue. ○ Depending on initial analysis of incident, assignment may be to a support group at the Service Desk (Incident Agent) or Tier 2 (Incident Analyst) • If the Incident Agent is not able to resolve the incident at the Service Desk, the incident may be dispatched to a Tier 2 / Incident Analyst for deeper investigation. This action will result in a subsequent assignment notification.	
Task: 3.0 Incident Status Notification	Role(s): Tool. User

Tasks Description: • Automated notifications sent out to user(s) and Service Desk advising of incident ticket status changes.	
Task: 4.0 Resolve Incident	**Role(s):** Incident Analyst

Tasks Description:
- Diagnosis and resolve incident.
- Advise Service Desk of significant updates/progress/delays.
- Update incident work log with resolution efforts
- Notify Service Desk of incident resolution.
- Change incident ticket status to Resolved / Fulfilled

Task: 5.0 SLA / OLA Not in compliance Notification	**Role(s):** Incident Agent

Tasks Description:
- 75% prior to and immediately following an SLA / OLA Not in compliance, notify operation support group of service level adherence situation.

Task: 6.0 Escalation 1	**Role(s):** Incident Coordinator

Tasks Description:
- Escalation of an incident can be triggered via the following methods:
  - Sev 1 = 25% of the SLA / OLA (30 minutes have passed / no significant progress achieved since receipt of user-initiated escalation)
  - Sev 2 = 50% of the SLA / OLA (60 minutes have passed / no significant progress achieved since receipt of user-initiated escalation)
  OR
  - Service Desk receives a user-initiated escalation request due to dissatisfaction with existing incident resolution performance.
- Upon receipt of notification, validate escalation request with Team Lead and Incident Coordinator
- Notification Contact:
  - Incident Manager
- Incident Manager reviews escalation details and assumes ownership of incident.
  - If required, Incident Manager engages the Incident Coordinator to coordinate and fulfill resolution activities.

Task: 6.1 Escalation 2	**Role(s):** Incident Manager

Tasks Description:
- Escalation 2 triggers:
  - Sev 1 = 50% of the SLA / OLA (60 minutes have passed / no significant progress achieved since receipt of user-initiated escalation)
  - Sev 2 = 75% of the SLA / OLA (2 hours have passed / no significant progress achieved since receipt of user-initiated escalation)
- Notification Contacts:
  - Team Leads
- Review and execute action plan as defined by Department Leads (if applicable)

Task: 6.2 Escalation 3	**Role(s):** Team Leads

Tasks Description:
- Escalation 3 triggers:
  - Sev 1 = 75% of the SLA / OLA (90 minutes have passed / no significant progress achieved since receipt of user-initiated escalation)
  - Sev 2 = SLA / OLA (3 hours have passed / no significant progress achieved since receipt of user-initiated escalation)
- Notification Contacts:
  - Management
- Review and execute action plan as defined by Management (if applicable)

Task: 6.3 Final Escalation	Role(s): Management

Tasks Description:
   • Escalation 4 triggers:
     ○ Sev 1 = SLA / OLA (over 90 minutes have passed / no significant progress achieved since receipt of user-initiated escalation)
   • Notification Contacts:
     ○ CIO
   • Review and execute action plan as defined by CIO (if applicable)	

Task: 7.0 Closure Notification	Role(s): Incident Agent

Tasks Description:
   • Engage user to confirm satisfaction with incident resolution.
   • Close incident ticket	

5.4 Criteria for Major Incident Declaration

5.4.1 Classification Framework

A Major Incident can be declared by the Incident Coordinator or the appropriate delegate at any time. The decision should be based on the results from the application of the following Major Incident classification framework.

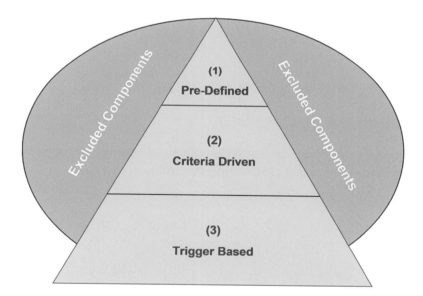

The **excluded components** are those that the Major Incident process will not handle the recovery efforts. Examples are:

1. Components issues arising from a project that is not part of the production environment.
2. Components issues arising from any application that is not part of the production environment.

Pre-Defined: This is a list of applications, systems, or services requiring a Major Incident to be declared if an unscheduled outage or degradation of service is experienced.

Criteria Driven: Collection of fundamental principles that function as guidelines for determining whether a Major Incident classification should be applied.

Major Incident Criteria	Example
IT Security Threat	Virus Outbreak
Core Operation Management Outage	Electronic mail Internet Intranet Windows Infrastructure (i.e. Active Directory) UNIX Infrastructure Site Power / HVAC Application inavalable (Banner, Ellipse, etc.)
Large Number of Users Affected	Head Office or Call Centre Identified critical locations or users

Trigger Based: Applicable for situations where Management has defined unique criteria for triggering the Major Incident process.

Management may request that an Incident which does not fall within the normal or pre-established criteria be treated as a Major Incident to ensure any of following activities is performed:

- Fan-out Incident Details to:
  o ITS Management
  o Business Area
- Communicate to the Client Community
- Create an Executive Briefing Note
- Conduct a Postmortem

The appropriate level of response will be evaluated on a case per case basis.

Extended or Repeated Outage or Service Degradation:

The initial incident did not align with Major Incident criteria but due to an extended or repeated service outage or degradation, the situation appears likely to be escalated to Management.

6   Process Role Mapping

6.1 RASCI Chart

The RASCI chart describes and defines the expectations for each person's role within the Incident Management Process. For every activity, within the process, the following has been determined:

RASCI Terminology	Activity
R – Responsible	✓ Responsible to take actions. ✓ The Prime mover à Coordinates work among support group. ✓ Ensure the work gets doneà the Doer. ✓ May also contribute to the actual work
A – Accountable	✓ Approves the action to be taken. ✓ Overseer of the work to be done ✓ Coordinates actions and direction ✓ Verifies work quality and completion. ✓ Obtains sign-off on deliverables
S – Support	✓ Supports the action. ✓ Provides support or resources
C - Consulted	✓ Consulted **before** the action is completed or delivered. ✓ Subject matter expert ✓ Provides input and recommends solutions. ✓ May influence the action
I – Informed	✓ Informed **after** the action is completed or delivered. ✓ Informed on a need-to-know basis on progress

NOTE: *the same person may be assigned to perform more than one role within the matrix*

RASCI Chart Ground Rules
1. No box should contain more than one letter 2. No more than one R should exist for any one action 3. The R should be placed first 4. As other letters are placed; the number of A's should be kept to a minimum

Process Activity	Incident Management Process Owner	Incident Manager	Incident Coordinator	Queue Manager	Incident Analyst	Incident Agent	User
1.0 Contact Service Desk	A						R
2.0 Log Incident		A				R	C
3.0 Perform First Level Diagnosis & Resolution		A		C		R	I
4.0 Dispatch and Monitor Incident	A					R	

5.0 Perform Second (nth) Level Diagnosis & Resolution		A		C	R	I	I
6.0 Manage Major Incident		A	R		C	I	I
7.0 Close Incident		A				R	C
8.0 Report Metrics	A	R					
9.0 Monitor Process	A	R					

Organizational Interrelationships

Incident Management Process Owner

- Interfaces primarily with the Incident Manager and other IT process stakeholders, who bring forward issues and requests to be dealt with at a process level, or for direction and guidance.
- Communicates incident process, roles & responsibilities, and policies.
- Is not typically involved in current service-related issues.

Incident Manager

- Escalates process issues and requests to Incident Management Process Owner
- Primary touch point for Service Desk, Team Leads, and Incident Coordinator for process issues, requests, and exceptions.
- Holds Incident Review Meetings with stakeholders.
- Receives and acts upon notifications and escalations issues by Incident Coordinator
- Facilitates Major Incident Postmortems with stakeholders.

Incident Coordinator

- Initiates the execution of the Major Incident process.
- Provides status and direction to Service Desk during Major Incidents
- Identifies and engages Incident Manager resources during Major Incidents
- Provides escalation and notifications to ITS Management during Major Incidents
- Schedules Major Incident Postmortems with stakeholders

Service Desk (Incident Agent)

- First Point of Contact (FPOC) for user as the intake process
- Notifies Incident Coordinator of potential 1, 2 incidents.
- Escalates unresolved incidents to Tier 2
- Participates in Incident Meetings

Queue Managers

- Ensure resolution of all assigned incidents
- Communicate resolution activities and workarounds to the Service Desk
- Participate in Major Incident meetings and activities as led by the Incident Manager
- Participates in Incident Meetings

7 Principles and Directives

7.1 Common Process Principles

- A standard Incident Management Process is defined to provide support to all ITS Service users.
- The Service Desk provides customers with a single point of contact for requesting incident support or IT service requests.
- The Service Desk opens, records, manages, tracks, escalates, closes, and communicates status of all incident records and is responsible for all incident assignments.
- The Incident Management Process is the conduit of communication of any degradation of service, to the affected users and IT personnel.
- Closure of incidents is dependent on validating with the user that the incident has been resolved and service is restored.
- There is a defined escalation process that ensures timely resolution of Incidents in compliance with Service Level Agreements and Operation Level Agreement (SLAs/OLAs).
- All incidents, as well as their solutions, are logged in an accessible Incident Management repository (?)
- All Service Providers will fulfill their roles in compliance with the ITS Incident Management process.
- Regularly scheduled process reviews will be conducted to improve the Incident Management processes.
- A new function is created to manage the overall incidents as the Incident Manager.

7.2 Ownership Directives

Ownership implies monitoring, communication coordination, escalation, updates, and resolution/fulfillment responsibility for both Service Interruption and Service Request incidents.

- When an incident is assigned, the Incident Analyst owns its resolution, which may involve communication with the end user.

7.3 Ticket Entitlement Directives

The ticket entitlement directive matrix follows:

Function	View	Change / Amend
Service Desk / Incident Manager / Coordinator	All records	All records
Queue Managers	All records assigned to their queue	All records assigned to their queue
Users	Only records opened by themselves or associated to those opened by themselves	None
Third Party	Assigned records	TBD
Team Leads	All records assigned to their team queues	All records assigned to their team queues

7.4 Major Incident Directives

- All Major Incidents affecting the Operation Management Production Environment will be handled by the ITS Major Incident process and will be managed under the respective standards, policies, and guidelines.
- The activity of recovering Major Incidents takes priority over all other tasks performed by all ITS staff.

- Regularly scheduled reviews of process components and contact information will be conducted to improve the Major Incident process execution.
- Incident Coordinator is the only resource authorized to validate the occurrence of and invoke the Major Incident process.
- Major Incidents are assigned to the Incident Coordinator immediately upon being changed to Resolved State, to prevent premature closing.

7.5 Incident Handling

7.5.1   Associations

Associating Incidents to Incidents

<u>Parent/Child</u>

Parent Record – A Parent record represents an incident where subsequent reporting of the same incident criteria is considered a repeat of the same underlying issue. Parent tickets are created when it is recognized that many calls may be received for the same service interruption. If the Parent Incident is resolved and the same issue recurs, a new Parent Incident will be generated for potential Childs to be associated to.

Child Record – A child record represents another user reporting the same service interruption as recorded in the parent, generally related to services having large customer base, i.e., network services, host services. Childs must have occurred during the duration of the Parent.

Creation of a Parent Incident Record

A Parent Record is created when it is recognized that multiple users will be calling in to report service interruptions that have been identified as being related to the same component failure. The Parent Record is assigned to the Support Group accountable for its resolution. All incidents logged for users experiencing the common impact are created as Childs to the Parent incident ticket.

Childs remain assigned to the Incident Agent who created the ticket. If it is deemed that direct user validation of resolution is not necessary, they will be resolved when the Parent is resolved.

The creation of a Parent Incident Record is an administrative convenience that serves the purpose to:

- Improve speed of logging incidents as Childs take on previously identified parent incident information.
- Simplify administration of major outages by focusing resources on parent incidents.
- Ensure completeness of incident information through replication of (some) updates.
- Improve accuracy of child incidents through replication of common information elements form the parent incident.
- Assist in defining the accuracy of impact of incidents by assessing geographic/services impacted extent).
- Improve reporting on major incidents by consolidating "like" incidents (Childs) to a single incident representing the overall outage. This provides information on the extent of the outage and ensures volume reporting is accurate, depending on the stakeholders need (e.g., volume of incidents important to Tier 1 for planning/re-sourcing, roll-up of Childs important to service owners/providers etc.).
- Prevent multiple incident tickets from being assigned to Tier 2, when they represent instances of the same component failure.

Duplicate

If multiple tickets are logged for a specific user, related to a specific issue, where the first occurrence was not resolved, the second ticket should be related to the first ticket and closed. This generally occurs when an Incident Agent does not review open tickets for a user before creating a new one.

Associating Incident to Change

- An incident directly resulting from a change – associate the incident with the change.
- A change resolving an incident – associate change to the incident.

Associating Incident to CI

<TO BE DEFINED>

Associating Incident to Problem

<TO BE DEFINED>

7.5.2 Incident Monitoring/Ownership

- Service Desk monitors the life cycle of the incident and has overall responsibility to ensure recovery is proceeding accordingly. If it is not proceeding accordingly, the IM is notified.

7.5.3 Reassignment Directives

- All incidents that are to be reassigned must go through the Service Desk unless the reassignment is specifically documented in a support procedure.
- Incidents that are reassigned more than three times will be reviewed by the Incident Manager, for efficiency purposes. Service Requests do not fall under this directive as reassignment may be procedural-ized.

7.5.4 Ticket Closure

- Upon resolving the incident, and prior to closure, the ticket owner must obtain confirmation from the user regarding the resolution.
- The only roles allowed to close an incident ticket are the Incident Agent, Incident Coordinator, and Incident Manager

7.5.5 Ticket Re-Open

- A closed incident ticket cannot be re-opened. If further investigation is required, a new incident record should be created and associated with the closed ticket.

8 Reference Data

8.1 Incident State Codes

Incident State	Description
New	The incident is in the process of being logged. In general, this state is provided to signify that the incident record is not yet complete and therefore, the incident resolution activity has not commenced.
Assigned	The incident has been assigned to a service provider in the service chain. The service provider may not accept the incident for action (move to In Progress) and may reassign the incident accordingly. In addition, it is possible that certain service providers (e.g., FPOC (First Point of Contact) at the service desk) may close the incident directly if the customer is not entitled to service.
Rejected	The assigned group has received the Incident and reviewed the content. The information required to proceed with the recovery of the Incident is not contained within the ticket. The ticket is marked as Rejected and is automatically placed in the Service Desk Queues requesting additional information. All Rejected tickets must have a detailed reason for the rejection.
In Progress	Incident restoration activities are progressing. This may include escalation of the incident to higher tiers of support, both internal and external to the organization.
Pending	Incident restoration activity is suspended, pending the fulfillment of customer dependent activities.
Resolved / Fulfilled	Service has been restored or a request has been fulfilled, from the service provider's perspective. Additional communication is required with the customer to confirm acceptance of the restoration. Restoration does not necessarily represent resolution of the problem that is causing the incident (if appropriate). It signifies that the customer can proceed with business activities, potentially through a workaround.
Closed	Incident management activity has concluded for the incident. No further updates are possible once an incident has been placed into this state.

The incident Assignee is required to provide updated incident record information each time the incident changes State. This is a minimum requirement and would require additional descriptions to be provided (i.e., Reason for State Change) in addition to the state change details. The specific date and time when the state was changed is also required in the communication, to account for system exchange delays.

8.2 Contact Code

When a contact is received, the Incident Agent must specify what type of contact is being registered. The following contact codes are defined:

Contact Code	Description
Phone	Incoming Phone, the Incident Agent receives a call by phone
E-Mail	Incoming email, the Incident Agent receives a contact by e-mail
Voice Mail	User unable to contact Incident Agent directly. Voice Mail is providing summarizing scope of request.
Walk Up	Incident Agent engaged via a local resource walk up

Web mail	User able to submit service request via web mail and may also check on their open Incident ticket only.
System Management	Automated event monitoring technology advises Incident Agent of Operation Management disruption

8.3 Incident Categorization

8.3.1 Impact, Urgency and Severity (Priority) Values

Incident Impact

Measure of scope and criticality to business. Often equal to the extent to which an incident leads to distortion of agreed or expected service levels. Impact is often measured by the number of people, critical systems affected or financial loss because of the service interruption. Incidents may default to a pre-defined impact based upon the Service Category, Component Category, and Incident Type.

Service Requests do not represent a business disruption, they represent a business need. As such, Service Requests default to a low impact.

Incidents must always reflect the highest actual impact identified during the initial diagnosis. If the impact of an incident is reduced, but not eliminated, the impact cannot be changed within the ticket. The only circumstance under which the impact can be lowered is if it is determined that it was incorrect in the first place.

The following impact codes are valid:

Impact	Description
High	Major business system or Operation Management failure affecting: • Public safety • Critical business application fully unavailable • $$$ quantified impact • All sites • Large customer groups
Medium	Business system or Operation Management failure affecting: • Public service • $$ quantified impact • Significant degradation in IT Service • Large group where work can continue. • Small group where work cannot continue (e.g., single office)
Low	Business system or Operation Management failure affecting: • Small group where work can continue. • Single user where work cannot continue, OR • Service Requests

Incident Urgency

Measures how quickly an incident needs to be responded to base on the business needs of the customer. Urgency is used by the Incident Agent and Incident Analyst to prioritize their workload; incidents with higher urgency will be addressed before others unless SLA breaches are imminent.

Currently, Incident Agents must manually determine the appropriate urgency for each incident. The intent is to define urgency for standard incidents, and for predefined High Impacts.

Service Requests that have specific turnaround times documented in SLAs will be given the urgency that corresponds to the agreed timeframe.

All staff and management will be treated as regular staff in the response and process execution.

Urgency	Description
High	The incident must be responded to immediately or a quickly as possible, all resources are to be focused on the resolution.
	Expedited Service Interruption; Senior Management: Legal or Regulatory.
Medium	The incident must be responded to in a timely fashion.
	Standard Service Interruption
Low	There is no formal urgency for response to the incident.
	Service Request

Severity

A combination of impact and urgency, used to generate a simplified value to drive escalation and notification.

		Impact		
		High	**Medium**	**Low**
Urgency	**High**	(1) Public Safety / Facing Company ABXYZ Safety Service Outages	(2) Public Service Internal Widespread/ Degradation	(3) High Sensitivity Incident Expedited Standard Incident Highly sensitive service Requests
	Medium	(1) Internal Impact	(2) Localized Core Operation Management Impact	(4) Standard Incident
	Low	(1) Impending Service Outage	(2) Impending Service Outage	(5) Service Request (6) Information Type (7) Other

The assigned Severity reflects the impact and urgency.

Assigning Impact and Urgency to Incidents

Incident Agents will assign Impact and Urgency.

In general:

- All Severity1 and 2 Incidents, the Incident Manager will be made aware. Based on assessment, may be handled by the Major Incident Process.
- All standard incidents will be logged as Impact=Low, Urgency=Medium, resulting in Severity 3 and 4
- All Service Requests should be logged as Impact=Low, Urgency= Low, resulting in Severity 5
- All Information type requests will be logged as Impact=Low, Urgency= Low, resulting in Severity 6

- All other type of requests will be logged as Impact=Low, Urgency= Low, resulting in Severity 7

The Severity assigned to an Incident represents the business impact, on Company ABXYZ, caused by the loss of a key service or asset. If the Severity is known at the time the Incident ticket is created, then it should be entered as such. If the Severity is not known at the time of the Incident, then a Severity 3 will be set. The Incident Manager will adjust the Severity based on the impact to the business. The new setting will be the default in any future Incident situations.

Incident Acknowledgement baseline

Currently, the direction is to use these as the baseline. However, these times can be changes when SLA is in place or as directed by management.

Severity Code	Queue Manager Acknowledgement Time Baseline
1	Core Hours - No more than 15 minutes
2	No More Than 2 Hours
3	No more than 4 Hours
4	No more than 2 Days
5	Agreed Timeframe
6	Agreed Timeframe
7	Agreed Timeframe

8.4 Resolution Category

Identifies the activity required to ultimately restore/fulfill service. The following Resolution Category values have been defined:

Resolution Category	Value	
Resolution Category – IT	**Advice Given -** *The user was provided with the information they requested (e.g., How-to, Information Request, Standard etc.).*	
	Resolved / Fulfilled - *The service has been restored or the request has been fulfilled accordingly.*	
	BY-PASSED	The service is restored by using established backup delivery procedures.
	FIXED	The resolution fixed the existing failing component.
	PREV FIX	An Incident search uncovered a previous incident resolution that fixed this incident. I.e., a known error.
	MATCH	The incident is closed and associated with a Parent incident having the same symptoms.

	Workaround Provided - *The user was able to resume activity through a workaround however the cause of the incident is still unknown and/or unresolved. The incident would be closed but may be associated to a problem.* **Duplicate -** *If multiple tickets are logged for a specific user, related to a specific issue, where the first occurrence was not resolved, the second ticket should be related to the first ticket and closed. This generally occurs when an Incident Agent does not review open tickets for a user before creating a new one.*
Resolution Category – User	**No Fault Found** - *Upon diagnosis, no incident was determined, and the customer was able to resume normal operations.* **Requester Cancelled** - *The user cancelled the request prior to incident resolution. (e.g., "It was my fault…")* **Not Entitled** - *The user is not entitled to service restoration or fulfillment activities. (e.g., have not purchased a specific level of service and therefore option x is not available, or the customer is not paying for the service in question).*

9 Process Metrics

Metrics are intended to provide a useful measurement of process effectiveness (The ability to achieve the desired objective) and efficiency (The results achieved versus resources used). Metrics are also required for strategic decision support.

Key Performance Indicators of the Incident Management process include:

- Quickly resolve Incidents.
- Maintain IT service quality.
- Improve business and IT productivity.
- User satisfaction

Roles associated with metrics:

Business	ITS service customer representative
Sr. IT Mgmt.	To be Entered by Organization.
IT Team Leads	IT Team Leads
Internal IT	Queue Managers

Please Note:

- Monthly metrics will be reported as a 13-month rolling report. Some of these reports may be part of OSR reporting.
- Each lead may have need of special reports. IF so, these can be obtained by contacting the Incident Manager on as needed basis.

9.1 Quickly Resolve Incidents

Service Interruption Metric	Target	Frequency	Audience
1. Mean response time (elapsed time) with number and percentage of Incidents handled within agreed to response target, by severity	As per section 7.3.1 of Process Guide	Monthly	Business
• By severity/queue	As per section 7.3.1 of Process Guide	Weekly	Sr. IT Mgmt.
• By severity/queue/analyst	As per section 7.3.1 of Process Guide	Weekly	IT Team Leads Internal IT
2. Mean recovery time (work effort or actual time) by severity (Parked – need to better define – Timesheet, reporting, Ellipse)	TBD	Monthly	Business Sr. IT Mgmt.

	Target	Frequency	Audience
• By severity/queue	TBD	Weekly	IT Team Leads
• By severity/queue/analyst	TBD	Weekly	Internal IT
3. Mean Time to Restore Service (MTRS) (elapsed time), with number and percentage of Incidents handled within agreed to recovery target, by severity	TBD	Monthly	Business Sr. IT Mgmt.
• By severity/queue	TBD	Weekly	IT Team Leads
• By severity/queue/analyst	TBD	Weekly	Internal IT
4. Ageing Incidents broken down by severity and queue	TBD	Monthly	Sr. IT Mgmt.
5. Ageing Incidents broken down by severity and queue (for weekly Incident meeting)	TBD	Weekly	IT Team Leads Internal IT
6. Time spent in Pending status – Min., Max. Avg., Trending	TBD	Weekly	IT Team Leads Internal IT

Service Desk Metric	Target	Frequency	Audience
1. Number and percentage of Incidents resolved on first call (need to create specific parameters)	TBD	Monthly	Sr. IT Mgmt.

9.2 Maintain IT Service Quality

Service Interruption Metric	Target	Frequency	Audience
1. Mean Time Between Failures (MTBF), by severity	TBD	Monthly	Sr. IT Mgmt. IT Team Leads Internal IT
2. Number and percentage of Incidents requiring a change in defined severity	TBD	Weekly (1st 2 months) then monthly	IT Team Leads Internal IT
3. Number and percentage of Incidents caused by Failed or 'In with Problem 'Change Requests (will identify issues either with the Change or the way it was communicated out to Users) (for Weekly Incident meeting). The Change Manager will report on Failed Changes or In with Problem. The Incident Manager will report on the incidents caused by these.	TBD	Weekly	IT Team Leads Internal IT
4. Number and percentage of Incidents escalated by the Service Desk	TBD	Monthly	Sr. IT Mgmt.
• By queue	TBD	Weekly	IT Team Leads
• By queue/analyst	TBD	Weekly	Internal IT
5. Number and percentage of Postmortem Reviews held within 48 hours with ageing of Postmortem Reviews still open broken down by queue	TBD	Monthly	Sr. IT Mgmt.
• By queue	TBD	Weekly	IT Team Leads Internal IT

	Target	Frequency	Audience
6. Number of improvement requests submitted, rejected, accepted, and implemented	No target	Monthly	Sr. IT Mgmt. IT Team Leads
7. Number of improvement requests ageing	TBD	Monthly	Sr. IT Mgmt. IT Team Leads
8. Average cost per Incident per channel (phone, e-mail, voice mail, walk up)	TBD	Monthly	Sr. IT Mgmt. IT Team Leads Internal IT

Service Desk Metric	Target	Frequency	Audience
1. Number and percentage of assignments that were rejected, by agent, queue, and CI (for Weekly Incident meeting)	TBD	Weekly	IT Team Leads Internal IT
2. Number and percentage of Incidents incorrectly escalated (as measured by rejected code)	TBD	Monthly	Sr. IT Mgmt.
• By CI/agent	TBD	Weekly	IT Team Leads Internal IT

9.3 Improve Business and IT Productivity

Service Interruption Metric	Target	Frequency	Audience
1. Number of Incidents recorded, broken down by severity and channel	TBD	Monthly	Business Sr. IT Mgmt.
• By queue and number of child Incidents	TBD	Weekly	IT Team Leads
• By queue/analyst and number of child Incidents	TBD	Weekly	Internal IT
2. Number of Incidents resolved, broken down by severity and queue	TBD	Monthly	Business Sr. IT Mgmt.
• By severity/queue	TBD	Weekly	IT Team Leads
• Broken down by severity/queue/analyst	TBD	Weekly	Internal IT
3. Number of Major Incidents, the number of Incidents which have evolved into Major Incidents, and the number of Major Incidents evolved to CERT	TBD	Monthly	Business Sr. IT. Mgmt.
• By queue/CI	TBD	Weekly	IT Team Leads Internal IT
4. Number of Major Incidents closed, percentage of Major Incidents which resulted in service restored within target time	TBD	Monthly	Sr. IT Mgmt.
• By queue/CI	TBD	Weekly	IT Team Leads Internal IT
5. Number and percentage of Incidents caused by security issues	TBD	Monthly	Sr. IT Mgmt. IT Team Leads Internal IT
6. Number and percentage of Incidents closed by Resolution code	TBD	Monthly	Sr. IT Mgmt.
• By queue	TBD	Weekly	IT Team Leads Internal IT

	Target	Frequency	Audience
7. Top 10 Incidents opened by CI, department, location	TBD	Monthly	Sr. IT Mgmt.
8. Top 5 Incidents opened by CI, department, location	TBD	Weekly	IT Team Leads Internal IT

Service Desk Metric	Target	Frequency	Audience
1. Number of calls received, and number of calls answered	No target	Monthly	Sr. IT Mgmt. IT Team Leads
2. Number and percentage of Incidents closed by the Service Desk without reference to other levels of support (service restored at first point of contact)	85%	Monthly	Sr. IT Mgmt. IT Team Leads
3. Number of Incidents and percentage of total processed per Service Desk Agent	TBD	Monthly	IT Team Leads
4. Average speed of answer for phone calls to Service Desk	85% in under <20 seconds	Monthly	Sr. IT Mgmt. IT Team Leads
5. Number of calls by interval and day of week per business unit	No target	Monthly	Sr. IT Mgmt. IT Team Leads
6. Number of abandoned calls by interval and day of week per business unit	No target	Monthly	Sr. IT Mgmt. IT Team Leads
7. Mean time to respond to Incident reported through email/voicemail (manual effort involved to collect this data)	TBD	Monthly	Sr. IT Mgmt. IT Team Leads

9.4 User Satisfaction

Service Interruption Metric	Target	Frequency	Audience
1. Number of User/Customer surveys sent/ responded to	TBD	Monthly	Sr. IT Mgmt.
2. Average User/Customer survey score (total and by question category)	85%	Monthly	Business Sr. IT Mgmt. IT Team Leads Internal IT
3. Number of Incidents created due to User complaints	TBD	Monthly	Sr. IT Mgmt. IT Team Leads Internal IT

Service Desk Metric	Target	Frequency	Audience
1. Number and percentage of calls abandoned (after 20 seconds)	<6% for calls waiting >20 seconds	Monthly	Sr. IT Mgmt. IT Team Leads

Service Level Management

An objective of the Service Level Management process is to ensure that services and levels of services agreed to with the customers are provisioned with the appropriate level of support and response by the performers of the Incident Management process.

The relationships between Incident Management and Service Level Management are:

- Services, as defined by Service Level Management, are related to Configuration Management (i.e., Configuration Items), and are represented in the Service Category field which is used by Incident Agents when logging tickets.
- Service Level Management provides Incident Management with defined incident and service request resolution times, which are applied in the SLM module and used to define target resolution times to be met by Incident Agents and Analysts
- Incident Management collects information required by Service Level Management to measure service delivery against agreed targets.
- Service Level Management will communicate, or market, to customers the service features, customer requirements, and levels of service for incident response and request handling.
- Service Level Management provides Incident Management with provisioning entitlement details for customers.

Configuration Management

The objective of Configuration Management process is to ensure correct and complete configuration information is available for resolution, research, analysis, and diagnosis of activities.

The relationships between Incident Management and Configuration Management are:

- IT assets, as defined by Configuration Management, are represented in the Component Category field which is used by Incident Agents when logging tickets.
- Services (Service Category) and People (Contacts) information is also provided to Incident Management via Configuration Management.
- The Incident Agents, when relevant to their other activities, verify configuration information in the database and report any discrepancies or errors.
- Configuration Management defines what can be changed by Incident Agents and/or Analysts.
- Configuration Management validates any changes made by Incident Agents and/or Analysts.
- The CMDB defines the relationships between resources, services, users, and Service Levels, thereby enabling support groups to assess impact, diagnose and resolve incidents.

Change Management

This process consists of all activities dealing with changes in the services and the IT Operation Management components they relate to.

The relationships between Incident Management and Change Management are:

- Incident Management identifies incidents that occur due to changes, allowing the Change Manager to assess the quality of the change.
- Incident Management generates changes that are required as part of the incident resolution.

- Change Management notifies the Service Desk of upcoming changes, via the established Change Management procedures in place, allowing staff levels to be adjusted accordingly.
- Change Management maintains current change status information to enable the Service Desk to provide accurate updates to customers.

Problem Management

This process is focused on defining and researching problems based on incident information. Statistical reports and trend analysis from the Incident Management process will provide a starting point for root cause analysis and identification of structural faults and errors in the supported IT Operation Management.

The relationships between Incident Management and the Problem Management process are:

- Incident Management collects information required by Problem Management to identify trends and issues.
- Problem Management provides temporary solutions and knowledge base information to support the Service Desk with incident restoration, allowing the analysts to restore service as quickly as possible.
- The management of the Major Incidents may be transferred to the Problem Management

11 Appendices

11.1 Incident Management Meetings

11.1.1 Weekly Incident Review Meeting

Description:

The purpose of the Weekly Incident Review meeting is to ensure that incidents are being addressed in a timely manner to achieve Service Level Targets, as well as to ensure that the Incident Management Process is being adhered to and is efficient and effective in execution. The Incident Manager provides an agenda before the meeting and distributes minutes after the meeting.

Meeting Format:

This is a round table discussion that includes:

- Reviewing open incidents – aging, high volume within each queue.
- Discussing specific incidents and resolutions as required
- Discussing any new tasks, action plans, issues or concerns and assigning ownership.
- Obtaining agreement to close incidents, for any in dispute.
- Reviewing Incident Management performance metrics monthly

The results of this meeting are to update the Incident Management System and provide minutes of the meeting to appropriate management.

Attendees:

- Incident Manager (Chairperson)
- Team Leads or delegate and Incident Agents (as appropriate) involved with active incidents.
- Incident Coordinator

Time and Place:

Weekly Meeting arranged by Incident Manager

Meeting Preparation:

- Review Incident Management reports

11.1.2 Major Incident Team Meeting

Description:

The Major Incident Team Meeting is an emergency meeting called when the diagnosis of an incident involves many players, the resolution is unknown, and efforts must be coordinated to ensure resolution. The incident details are discussed, and immediate actions are assigned to revive the service.

Meeting Format:

This is a round table discussion that includes:

- Reviewing incident cause and history
- Discussing corrective actions to regain the service.
- Assigning resources and performing an immediate action plan

Running the Major Incident Team (MIT):

- Follow the existing "Major Incident Checklist".
- Assemble the existing chronology of the incident as documented in the related incident record/case(s)
- Determine Business impact and establish its importance within the context of the relevant Service Level Agreement (SLA), if one is in place.
- Understand the incident and the full impact of the related action(s) taken and balance the risk of premature action versus the need to restore services.
- Manage the MIT, set the agenda and follow existing processes.
- Keep the focus of all participants on the recovery of service by encouraging participation of all MIT members. Discourage any "blaming" or "fault finding" between members.

Assign a scribe, which may be the Incident Coordinator, to record the proceedings but remain responsible for the content. The scribe should be familiar with the terminology and can adequately articulate the proceedings of the MIT in minutes (Incident Coordinator). Determine action plans to recover from the incident and document possible alternatives.

- Co-ordinate resources and be aware of any other MIT in-progress. They could be related.
- Determine when a normal or controlled processing environment established and conduct a final status review prior to releasing the MIT members.
- Notify the Incident & Change Management Manager when an MIT has been held. Provide necessary information on the incident along with the related incident record/case(s) prior of the MIT breaking up, or the next morning.

Attendees:

- Incident Manager (Chairperson)
- Incident Coordinator
- All staff involved.

Time and Place:

Called by the Incident Coordinator (based on input from Incident Manager) on an as needed basis. However, every effort should be made to have a dedicated "War Room" as a centralized place to conduct the MIT meeting.

Meeting Preparation:

- None

11.1.3 Postmortem

Description:

The objective of the Postmortem meeting is to ensure that the chronology of events related to a Major Incident is documented accurately, identify any delays or issues related to non-compliance in the process or shortcomings in the process, make recommendations for preventing reoccurrences, and advise on any continuous improvement opportunities.

Meeting Format:

This is a round table discussion about the incident(s).

- Review all the facts about the incident.
- Discuss preventative actions and alternatives.
- Create a plan to put new measures in place.
- Get commitment on resources.
- Assign tasks to resources.

Attendees:

- Incident Coordinator (Chairperson)
- Incident Manager
- Service Desk Team Lead
- Severity 1 team participants (as required)
- Change Manager
- Optional Participants:
  - Customer and / or User
    - Note: *Due to sensitivity of potential discussion content, core team should be consulted prior to inviting Customer / User to Postmortem session*

Time and Place:

The Postmortem must be held within 48 hours (i.e., 2 business days) of the resolution of the Major Incident. This time frame must be met to

a) ensure that the details of the incident are fresh in the participant's minds, and
b) to ensure that a timely report is submitted to the customer impacted.

Participation in a Postmortem Review is mandatory. If for any reason any of the participants are unable to attend, they are accountable for.

a) notifying the Incident Coordinator in advance of the meeting, and
b) arranging for another representative, familiar with Major Incident, to attend.

If all required participants are not available, the Postmortem review will be rescheduled possibly resulting in the 2-business day timeframe being missed.

Meeting Preparation:

Incident Manager or Incident Coordinator prepares a draft postmortem report based upon the content of the incident record and issues to all expected participants with meeting invitation.

11.2 Postmortem Templates

11.2.1 Consolidated Major Incident List Template

Date Initiated	tool Incident #	Description	Date Resolved	Major Incident Process Checklist Completed (Y/N)	Postmortem Completed (Y/N)	Total # of Action Items/ Recommendations	Total # of Outstanding Action Items

11.2.2 Major Incident Action Item Tracking Log Template

Date	Incident #	Recommendations / Action Item	Business Impact if not addressed	Raised By	Responsible Manager	Assignee	Detailed Analysis Completed (Y/N)	Cost Involved	Staff Resources	Management Decision Required	Due Date	Completed Date	Notes	Date that Incident Manager presented to Mgmt.

Note: The Incident Manager is the owner and will provide the location of the completed template to all affected parties.

11.2.3 Postmortem Report Template

Major Incident Postmortem Report
for Incident # nnnnn

Incident Coordinator:
Jane Doe
ITS Service Desk
Phone: 555-555-5555

Incident Manager:
John Doe
Phone: 555-555-5555

Incident:	*Incident Description*
Date/Time of Incident:	*dd/mm/yy hh:mm*
Current Status:	*State dd/mm/yy hh:mm (when state was entered)*
Duration of Outage:	*nn hours nn minutes*
Incident Ticket:	
○ **Created - Date/Time:**	*dd/mm/yy hh:mm*
○ **Resolved - Date/Time:**	*dd/mm/yy hh:mm*
○ **Duration of Ticket:**	*nn hours nn minutes*
Incident Occurrence:	
○ **Started – Date/Time:**	*dd/mm/yy hh:mm*
○ **Restored – Date/Time:**	*dd/mm/yy hh:mm*
○ **Duration of Incident:**	*nn hours nn minutes*
Business Impacts:	*In business terms:* *describe how the service is used and by whom.* *what functions could not be performed?* *estimated loss of productivity or other financial impacts* *public credibility or service impact* *Customer Service will provide input and/or confirmation of this information.*
Failing System or Component	*Current Component Category*
Resolution Activity	*Resolution free form field*
Associated Incidents	*Identify any associated incidents and describe relationship*
Previous Occurrences	*Identify if this is a recurring Major Incident*
Root Cause Analysis?	*Requirement to be established based on defined criteria*
Summary of Events:	*(Summarize work log and assignment tab – preference to not cut and paste)*
hh:mm	*event*
hh:mm	*event*
hh:mm	*event*
hh:mm	*event*
hh:mm	*event*
hh:mm	*event*

#	Issues / Recommendations	Action Item #
1		
2		
3		
4		

#	Action Item	Assigned to	Next Update	Status
1				
2				
3				
4				

Attachments: *Incident record, analysis reports, other pertinent documents*

11.2.4 Major Incident Checklist

#	Checklist	Yes	No	Date & Time Completed	Exception Comments
1	Potential Major Incident Identified				
2	Validate Major Incident Occurrence with Incident Manager				
3	Severity 1 Ticket Opened/Upgraded				
4	Fan Out to ITS Stake Holders via Approved Messaging				
5	If required, issue Briefing Note to Affected Business units and CIO Office				
6	Communicate Incident to ITS Service Desk				
7	Update ITS Service Desk IVR Phone)				Ensure IVR is updated following significant status change
7.2	Issue Notification to MIT team				
8	Issue Client Communication to Impacted Clients				
9	Issue Updated Approved Messaging to ITS Stake Holders Every 3 hours or upon Significant Status Change				
10	Issue Updated Communication to Clients Every 3 hours or upon Significant Status Change				
11	Check Point Meeting with Technical Team				
12	Incident Resolution Confirmed				
13	Issue Resolution Fan Out to ITS Stake Holders via Approved Messaging				
14	Communicate Resolution to Clients				
15	Severity 1 Ticket Closed				
17	Conduct Postmortem Review Meeting				
18	Determine if Root Cause Analysis is Required				
19	Document Postmortem Report				
20	Distribute Validated Postmortem Report to Mgmt. & Technical Team				
21	Perform Quality Assurance on Major Incident Checklist				
22	Save Completed Major Incident Checklist on Common Repository				

11.3 Major Incident Notification Templates

11.3.1 Service Status Messaging

SERVICE INTERRUPTION NOTICE

Service Affected:	Enter the name of the service affected.
Description:	Identify who is affected, and where the affected area is located.
Date:	Exact date the interruption occurred.
Time:	List when the interruption started.
Duration:	Provide the estimated up-time.
Impact:	A general description of the interruption and business impact if available along with any action the recipient is required to take.
Contact:	If you have any questions or concerns, please contact the **Help Desk@ 12345**

SERVICE AVAILABILITY NOTICE

Service Affected:	Name of the service that was down
Description:	Define the service that was recovered and identify if any or all components have been recovered of there are still some to be recovered.
Date:	Date the recovery occurred.
Time:	Time the recovery occurred.
Impact:	Provide the status of the recovery or if the user is expected to do something not part of their standard access to be able to use the service.
Contact:	If you have any questions or concerns, please contact Help Desk@ 12345

11.3.2 Service Desk IVR Broadcast

Purpose:	To inform all callers to the ITS Service Desk of the occurrence and resolution status of a Major Incident.
Document Structure:	The IVR broadcast message represents a brief high-level statement of the Major Incident occurrence.
	Service(s) Affected: List of all clients facing services affected by the Major Incident.
	Clients Impacted: List the clients impacted by the Major Incident.
	Hours of Operation: Indicate the hours of operation for the Service Desk.
	Time Stamp: Indicate the date and time of both the Major Incident occurrence and issuing of the IVR broadcast message.
Comments:	

Example:	Thank you for calling the ITS Service Desk.

Attention: As of Monday January 28 1:30 pm, Email service at 14 Carlton is currently unavailable. ITS is working on a resolution and will update this message when services have been restored.

Our hours of operation are 7:30 AM - 6 PM, Monday - Friday.

11.3.3 Management Notification (Approved Messaging)

Purpose: Provide the CIO Office and the Management Team with prompt notification of a Major Incident occurrence and regular updates on the resolution progress.

Document Structure: Given the management audience for this notification, the content should be relatively high-level, contain minimal acronyms, and focus on the business impact. The content is to be authored in a multi paragraph form.

Service(s) Affected: List of all clients facing services affected by the Major Incident.

tool Ticket #: Reference Incident ticket #.

Vendor Ticket #: If applicable, reference any associated vendor ticket #.

Clients Impacted: If applicable, list the clients impacted by the Major Incident.

Assigned Support Resources: List the support resources that have been engaged to resolve the Major Incident.

Incident Coordinator Contact Info: Provide contact information for the Incident Coordinator.

11.3.4 Briefing Note

Purpose: To ensure the CIO is made aware and provided with timely information throughout the duration of a Major Incident.

Document Structure: Within the Briefing Note, there are three primary sections. The document should have minimal "technical jargon", void of acronyms, and be understandable by the business.

Issue: Brief synopsis of the scope and impact of the Major Incident.

Current Status: Summary of the current state of the Major Incident and the resolution efforts performed to date.

Background: Overview of the events, systems, resources, and locations that contributed towards the occurrence of the Major Incident.

11.3.5 Client Communication Template

Purpose: To ensure all applicable ITS Clients are informed of a Major Incident and status of on-going resolution efforts.

Document Structure: The Client Communication E-Mail should avoid technical terminology and be authored at a level which compliments the client's knowledge and perception of the affected service.

Service Outage Description: Brief explanation of the Major Incident situation and any significant resolution efforts being performed. Contingency or mitigation efforts to minimize the impact of the incident should be communicated if applicable.

Site(s) Impacted: List of all the sites affected by the Major Incident.

Service(s) Affected: List of all clients facing services affected by the Major Incident.

Service(s) Not Affected: List of relevant clients facing services not affected by the Major Incident.

Service Desk Contact #: 1-800-?????????

Temporary Workaround: If available, advise of a temporary workaround the client can invoke to minimize the impact of the Major Incident

Comments:
- Flag E-Mail as a "High" priority within GroupWise
- Ensure E-Mail sent from the "Service Desk" mailbox.
- Following the initial Client Communication E-Mail, all future notifications must contain a log of all previously issued communication text.

11.4 Glossary

Term	Description
Asset Management	A standard accounting process concerned with maintaining the details of assets above a specified value, including depreciation, lease agreement information, expected life, etc. Asset management does not track the relationship between assets and may not track each individual item purchased or leased as part of a "bundle" purchase. (For example, asset management would track the fact that 100 personal computers were purchased but would not track the individual units.) Configuration Management would typically track the individual PCs.
Availability	Ability of a component or service to perform its required function at a stated instant or over a stated period. Generally, availability is expressed as the availability ratio, which is the proportion of time that the service is available for use by the Customers within the agreed service hours.
Availability Management	A process that focuses on understanding and managing availability requirement of the business.
Change Advisory Board (CAB)	An advisory committee that provides expert advice to the change manager on change issues
Capacity Management	A process that aims at ensuring that the capacity of the IT Operation Management matches current and future requirements of the business.
Category	Classification - possibly based on nature of event.
Change	Any modification – addition or removal of approved, supported, or base lined hardware, network, software, application, environment, system, desktop build or associated documentation.
Change Management	Process of implementing Changes to the Operation Management or any aspect of services, in a controlled manner, enabling approved Changes with minimum disruption to service.
CI (Configuration Item)	Component of IT Operation Management or a related item under the control of Configuration Management.
Configuration Baseline	A snapshot of the IT Operation Management as recorded in the CMDB. Although the snapshot may be updated later, as changes are applied to CIs, the baseline remains unchanged and available as a reference of the original state and as a comparison against the current state.
Configuration Management	A process for identifying, recording, auditing, and reporting on the CIs for accuracy and completeness.
Configuration Management Database (CMDB)	A database containing the relevant details of each CI and details of the important relationships between CIs.
Configuration Management Plan	Document describing the organization and procedures for the Configuration Management of a specific project, product, system, support group or service.
Contingency Planning	The preparation to address unwanted occurrences that may happen later. Usually, the term has been used to refer to planning for the recovery of IT systems rather than entire business processes.
Continuity Management	A process that supports the Business Continuity process to ensure that IT Services are recovered within agreed time scale.

Term	Description
Crises Management	An occurrence and / or perception that threatens the operations, staff, shareholder value, stakeholders, brand, reputation, trust and / or strategic / business goals of an organization.
Customer	Recipient of a service, responsible for funding the service against business requirements.
CSB	Corporate Security Branch
Customer Management	Customer Management process establishes and maintains links between executive business managers and the IT services organization.
Definitive Hardware Store (DHS)	Definitive Hardware Store. An area that is aside for the secure storage of definitive hardware spares.
Definitive Software Library (DSL)	Definitive Software Library. A secure software library where all versions of accepted software configuration items (CIs) are held in their definitive, quality-controlled form.
Disaster recovery planning	Set of processes that focus only on the recovery processes, mainly in response to the physical disasters, which are contained within BCM.
Domain Name System (DNS)	Distributed, static database the Internet uses to translate 32-bit IP addresses into domain names. Each time a domain name is used, a DNS service translates the name into the corresponding IP address.
Emergency Change Advisory Board (ECAB)	A subset of the CAB that is always available to be called upon to address emergency or urgent change issues
End User (or User)	The individual who uses the service on a day-to-day basis.
Forward Change Schedule	A schedule of all approved changes and their planned implementation dates for a pre-specified period.
IDS	Intrusion Detection System
Impact	Measure of scope and criticality to business.
Incident	An event that negatively impacts the standard delivery of a service, or a service request
Incident Management	A process that is committed to restoring normal service operations as documented in Service Level Agreements as well as processing service requests.
IT Service Delivery	IT Service Delivery processes (Availability Management, Capacity Management, Continuity Management, Financial Management and Service Level Management) address from a design and management perspective the service that business requires of the provider.
Known Error	An incident or Problem for which the root cause is known and for which a temporary Work-around or a permanent alternative has been identified. If a business case exists, an RFC will be raised, but, in any event, it remains a known error unless it is permanently fixed by a change.
Maintainability	Describes the ability of the Internal IT groups to maintain the services via the management of IT Operation Management components or services. Managed through OLAs.
Mean Time Between Failures (MTBF)	Expected future performance based on the actual past performance of a population of units. Calculated as: (MTBF = total actual operating time / total number of failures).
Mean Time to Repair (MTTR)	Average amount of time it takes to repair a component. MTTR typically includes time from when the unit failed until replaced, thus including hardware unavailability, response time, travel time, and on-site repair time.

Term	Description
Metric	A measurable element of the service process or function.
Operational Level Agreement	An internal agreement covering the delivery of services, which support the IT organization in their delivery of services.
Operational Test Environment	A test environment that is directly used by customers or end-users as part of the IT services they receive.
Operations Management	A process that consists of all activities and measures necessary to enable and maintain the intended use of IT services and production environment.
PKI	Public Key Infrastructure
Post Implementation Review	A review for verification of correct implementation of change by authorized personnel.
Priority	Relative order in which a given event needs to be addressed. This usually depends on Impact and Urgency.
Problem	An unknown underlying cause which could or has caused disruption of service.
Problem Management	A process that minimizes the effect of errors in Operation Management / services and external events on the customers. It is a process focused on diagnosing and rectifying faults in the IT Operation Management to obtain the highest possible IT service stability.
Procedure	A set of specific steps that describe how an activity should be carried out, and by whom. Procedures may be supported by more detailed Work Instructions. A Process defines what is to be achieved; Procedures define how the objectives are to be achieved.
Process	A series of related activities aimed at achieving a set of objectives (or Policies) in a measurable, usually repeatable, manner. It will have defined information inputs and outputs, will consume resources and will be subject to Management controls over time, cost, and quality. It will also balance benefits against risks.
Process Owner	The Process Owner is the person involved in the project regarding process design and / or re-engineering efforts.
Production environment	A subset of IT Operation Management that participates in delivery of Service.
RASCI Matrix	RASCI diagrams are tools used to map activities to roles and define how roles contribute to an activity.
Release	A collection of new or changed CIs.
Release to Production	The process, which controls the release of changes in the production IT Operation Management. It is a component of the ITIL Release Management Process.
Reliability	The service or IT Operation Management Configuration Item (CI) is available when expected / as defined in the SLA. It can also be described as freedom from failure. It is expressed in terms of MTBF - average uptime.
Request for Change (RFC)	Form, or screen, used to record details of a request for a change to any CI within an infrastructure or to procedures and items associated with the infrastructure.
Resilience	Degree redundancy of a CI with the intent of eliminating single points of failure in the Operation Management.
Security Incidents	Security incidents are those events that cause damage to confidentiality, integrity or availability of information or information processing and materialize as accidents or deliberate acts.
Service Catalogue	Written statement of IT services, default levels and options.

Term	Description
Service Delivery	Processes that address Service Management from a design and management perspective.
Service Desk	Single point of contact between Service Provider and the users of the Service.
Service Improvement Program	A formal project undertaken within an organization to identify and introduce measurable improvements within a specified work area or work process.
Service Level Agreement (SLA)	Written agreement between a service provider and the Customer(s), that documents agreed Service Levels for a Service. The scope of an SLA covers the target environment to be serviced, specific IT service deliverables, service functionality, service coverage (e.g., level, hours, availability, responsiveness, restrictions, authorizations, etc.), security policies, and cost of the services being provide the respective roles of IT and the business unit for on-boarding, training, end user support etc.
Service Level Management	A process that defines Service levels agreed with customer and subsequently manages at an acceptable cost.
Service Level Objective (SLO)	A defined target for a service metric, usually specified in an SLA.
Service Management	Management of Services to meet the Customer's requirements.
Service Planning	The Service Planning process designs, develops and controls Service Plan required for service development. This plan will describe scope, functional requirements and required components for service implementation that aids in determination of service ROI along with decisions like "Buy Vs Build".
Service provider	Third-party organization supplying services or products to customers.
Service quality plan	The written plan and specification of internal targets designed to guarantee the agreed service levels.
Service Request	Every Incident not being a failure in the IT Operation Management.
Serviceability	Describes the external contracts or Underpinning Contracts (UCs) that exist with suppliers that are required to deliver service.
Services	The deliverables of the IT Services organization as perceived by the Customers; the services do not consist merely of making computer resources available for customers to use.
Severity	The business impact caused at the time the service interruption occurred OR realized by the recipient of the service.
TIER	A row or rank that is dependent on each other for support. The lowest tier will support the above as so on. I.e., Tier 1 will support Tier 2, etc.
Underpinning contract	A contract with an external supplier covering delivery of services that support the IT organization in their delivery of services.
Urgency	Measures how quickly an event needs to be addressed.
Workaround	Restoring service by application of temporary fix or routing service to the customer via another channel.
Workgroup	An organizational or logical unit of individuals with similar specialization and responsibilities

11.5 Document Quality Control Process

Routine reviews of the Incident Management process will be performed by the Incident Process Owner, Incident Manager, and other key stakeholders. Performance reports and customer satisfaction surveys should be leveraged as key feedback mechanisms. This will enable effective assessments of the quality and integrity of the process, verify alignment with business objectives, and minimize resource or ownership issues. If required, continuous improvement initiatives can then be formulated to further refine and optimize the process, as per following:

11.6 Continuous Improvement activities

• **APPROACH**
As a team, the Process Owners/Incident Manager will periodically review the Incident Management Process to determine whether it continues to facilitate quality resolution and increase customer satisfaction. Involving all the participants (Incident Manager, Coordinator and Queue Managers) is critical in its analysis
• **OBJECTIVE REVIEW**
Review the Incident Management processes' objective. What are its goals, metrics to achieve, activities performed. Identify the key performance objectives to achieve and validate of planned versus actual result and address any anomalies.
• **MAPPING**
Process maps are especially effective when relationships are complex, and several tasks occur simultaneously. Using the Incident Management Process Guide, it identifies the critical paths that will allow the team to track activities
• Analyze the operations performed in their area.
• Review the processes and Work Instructions that must be accomplished
• Identify both the formal processes and the way things are really done.
• Identify the decision-makers and the key communication points.
• Include people both inside and outside the unit who are involved in the Incident Management process
• **ROLES and RESPONSIBLITIES**
• Study the Incident Management current structure, such as who reports to whom and what their responsibilities are.
• Which elements of this design no longer serve a purpose
• Was the structure built around the capabilities of persons or tools that no longer exist?
• Refine roles and responsibilities in the RASCI format.
• **DIAGNOSE**
• Identify what is working and what is not.
• Identify bottlenecks and recurring incidents
• Note places where formal process is circumvented. Highlight internal and external user service incidents. Examine the level at which decisions are made.
• Identify duplication of effort
• Include what is working well. Examine why (lesson learned).
• Include what is not working and why?

• **IMPROVE**
As you analyze the Incident Management process, you can eliminate or modify inefficient activities and create new approaches. Use these steps to generate and analyze new alternatives. It is critical you work as a team when identifying new approaches.
• Identify activities the team find outdated, overly time consuming or redundant.
• Find out the purpose of the activity
• Evaluate the activity in detail, whether it is necessary or could be eliminated or combined with another activity.
• Generate as many alternatives as possible that would meet the same objectives.
• Review the potential alternatives and identify the superior solution
• Set-up a system to evaluate how well the solution really works within the process. Continue to evaluate it for improvement
• Ask the team to troubleshoot the incident areas and make recommendations.
• **RESEARCH**
Research Incident Management processes used in other organizations. Find out how their work processes are set up, what works well and what doesn't and why.
• **MAINTAIN**
Continue to clarify responsibilities and procedures through team meetings and other communication, vehicles. Set aside time during Incident Review meetings to discuss changes or improvements to the process.
• **STANDARDIZE**
If you standardize your Work Instructions in the process, you will not have to 'reinvent the wheel ' for each new department involved or for different kinds of situations or users. Instead, you can modify the Work Instructions to fit each new initiative.
• **AUTOMATE**
Technological improvements that meet the needs of the process can significantly increase efficiency, control and management in many cases, the cost of technology is quickly paid back through productivity increases.
Consider:
• Trending and statistical tools
• Incident diagnostic Systems
• Specific solutions such as:
✓ Documentation Repository
✓ System monitoring and auto Incident generators

12 Attachment

12.1 Incident Management Metrics Samples

These sample reports are indicative of the layout and content to be expected with other reports.

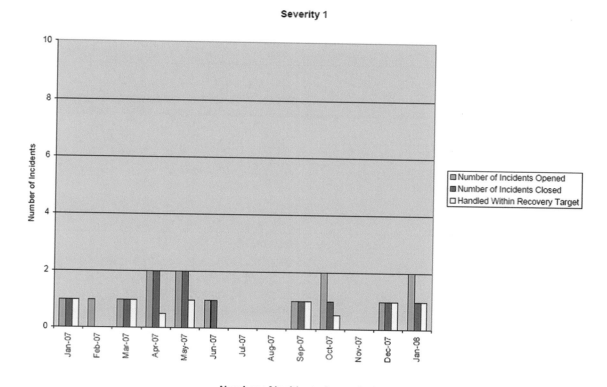

Severity 1

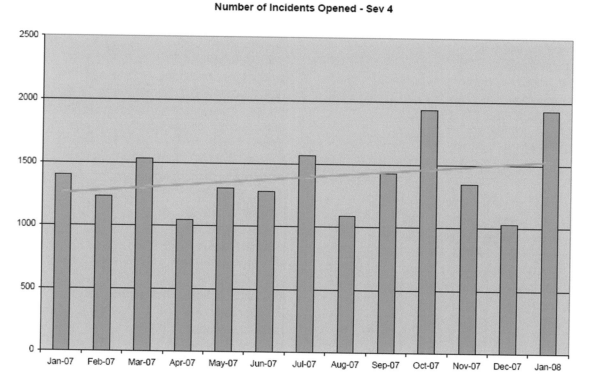

Number of Incidents Opened - Sev 4